Agape

Songs of Hope and Reconciliation

Lieder der Hoffnung und Versöhnung

Chants d'Espérance et de Réconciliation

Cantos de Esperanza y Reconciliación

Compiled by Maggie Hamilton and Päivi Jussila

MUSIC DEPARTMENT

OXFORD
UNIVERSITY PRESS

in association with
The Lutheran World Federation

on the occasion of
The LWF Tenth Assembly

OXFORD
UNIVERSITY PRESS

Great Clarendon Street, Oxford OX2 6DP, England
198 Madison Avenue, New York, NY10016, USA

Oxford University Press is a department of the University of Oxford.
It furthers the University's aim of excellence in research, scholarship,
and education by publishing worldwide in

Oxford New York
Auckland Bangkok Buenos Aires Cape Town Chennai
Dar es Salaam Delhi Hong Kong Istanbul Karachi Kolkata
Kuala Lumpur Madrid Melbourne Mexico City Mumbai Nairobi
São Paulo Shanghai Taipei Tokyo Toronto

Oxford is a registered trade mark of Oxford University Press
in the UK and in certain other countries

1 3 5 7 9 10 8 6 4 2

ISBN 0–19–100013–2

Music and text origination by
Barnes Music Engraving Ltd., East Sussex
Printed in Great Britain on acid-free paper by
Halstan & Co. Ltd., Amersham, Bucks.

Contents

Preface

by the Rev. Dr. Ishmael Noko, LWF General Secretary

The first Christians gathered around the table in order to eat, celebrate, witness, pray, and be strengthened in Christian faith. 'Agape', the title of this songbook, refers to these fellowship meals, these love feasts. It is with great pleasure that I present to you this book, introduced at the Tenth Assembly of the LWF, held in Winnipeg, Canada, 21–31 July 2003. The Assembly offers participants an opportunity to gather around the table in order to eat, praise, and share their experiences of love and healing.

The Greek word 'agape' (literally 'love') describes the universal, all-embracing love which flows from God. It is not an abstract concept. Rather, it refers to a way of life, characterized by justice, compassion, mutual respect, hospitality, service, reconciliation, and hope. The primary location of agape is *koinonia*, the community of the faithful, sustained by God's love.

Agape is not grounded in the lovableness of the person who is loved. Rather, it is love based on self-sacrifice and self-giving. It presupposes a radical change in one's way of relating to God, to one another, to oneself, and to nature. It involves a change in one's way of seeing, tasting, and hearing. The songs contained in this collection encourage and promote varied ways and expressions of seeing, crying, tasting, and praising. Love is expressed not only in holy words of wisdom or in the language of the angels. It is also whispered, murmured, and cried out in the language of the poor, the needy, and the oppressed. I believe that the variety of expression is vital to us as a communion. Through this kind of sharing and exchange we become truly ourselves. These songs of praise and lament from around the world help us to reconcile and to break down social, cultural, economic, gender, and racial barriers. They are not only *about* healing but are healing in themselves.

This songbook is a Lutheran contribution to the ecumenical and liturgical movement. It is my hope that after the Assembly it will be used worldwide at Lutheran and ecumenical gatherings as well as in local multicultural settings. The songs have been collected and selected by a number of representatives from the LWF member churches with ecumenical representatives.* I would like to thank this group, many additional consultants, and the Oxford University Press for their contribution to the life of the Assembly.

* Júlio Cézar Adam, Joy Berg, Marc Chambron, Per Harling, Stephen Larson, Terry MacArthur, Simei Monteiro, Jimson Sanga, Scott Weidler, Dietrich Werner, Mabel Wu, Päivi Jussila (coordinator).

Vorwort

von Pfr. Dr. Ishmael Noko, Generalsekretär des LWB

Die ersten ChristInnen versammelten sich um den Tisch um zu essen, zu feiern, Zeugnis abzulegen, zu beten und sich im christlichen Glauben stärken zu lassen. „Agape", der Titel dieses Liederbuchs, verweist auf diese gemeinschaftlichen Mahle, diese Liebesfeiern. Es ist mir eine grosse Freude Ihnen dieses Buch vorlegen zu können, das bei der Zehnten Vollversammlung des LWB in Winnipeg, Kanada, vom 21. bis 31. Juli 2003 eingeführt wird. Die Vollversammlung gibt den Teilnehmenden die Gelegenheit, um den Tisch zusammenzukommen um zu essen, Gott zu loben und ihre Erfahrungen der Liebe und Heilung auszutauschen.

Das griechische Wort *agape* (wörtlich „Liebe") beschreibt die universale, alles umfassende Liebe, die von Gott ausgeht. Dies ist kein abstraktes Konzept. Vielmehr verweist der Begriff auf einen Lebensstil, der von Gerechtigkeit, Mitgefühl, gegenseitiger Achtung, Gastfreundschaft, Dienst, Versöhnung und Hoffnung geprägt ist. Agape ist vorrangig angesiedelt in der *koinonia*, der Gemeinschaft der Gläubigen, die erhalten wird von Gottes Liebe.

Agape beruht nicht auf der Liebenswürdigkeit der Person, die geliebt wird. Sie ist vielmehr eine Liebe, die in Selbstaufopferung und Selbsthingabe gründet. Sie setzt eine radikale Veränderung in der Art voraus, wie eine Person in Beziehung steht zu Gott, anderen Menschen, sich selbst und der Natur. Dazu gehört eine Veränderung der Art und Weise, wie man sieht, schmeckt und hört. Die Lieder dieser Sammlung ermutigen und regen an zu unterschiedlichen Weisen und Formen des Sehens, Klagens, Schmeckens und Lobpreisens. Liebe wird nicht nur in heiligen Worten der Weisheit oder in der Sprache der Engel ausgedrückt. Sie wird auch geflüstert, gemurmelt und geschrien in der Sprache der Armen, Notleidenden und Unterdrückten. Meiner Ansicht nach ist diese Vielfalt der Ausdrucksformen lebensnotwendig für uns als Gemeinschaft. Durch dieses Teilen und diesen Austausch werden wir wahrhaft wir selbst. Diese Lieder des Lobpreises und der Klage aus aller Welt helfen uns, zu versöhnen und Schranken sozialer, kultureller, wirtschaftlicher Unterschiede sowie der Unterschiede des Geschlechts und der Hautfarbe niederzureissen. Sie handeln nicht nur *von* Heilung, sondern *sind* selbst Heilung.

Dieses Liederbuch ist ein lutherischer Beitrag zur ökumenischen und liturgischen Bewegung. Ich hoffe, dass es nach der Vollversammlung bei lutherischen und ökumenischen Versammlungen sowie in lokalen multikulturellen Kontexten Verwendung finden wird. Die Lieder wurden von einer Reihe von VertreterInnen aus den LWB-Mitgliedskirchen und der Ökumene gesammelt und ausgewählt*. Ich möchte dieser Gruppe und vielen weiteren Einzelpersonen, die geholfen haben, sowie Oxford University Press für ihren Beitrag zu einer lebendigen Vollversammlung danken.

* Júlio Cézar Adam, Joy Berg, Marc Chambron, Per Harling, Stephen Larson, Terry MacArthur, Simei Monteiro, Jimson Sanga, Scott Weidler, Dietrich Werner, Mabel Wu, Päivi Jussila (Koordinatorin).

Avant-propos

du pasteur Ishmael Noko, secrétaire général de la FLM

Les premiers(ères) chrétien(ne)s se réunissaient autour d'une table pour manger, célébrer, témoigner, prier et affirmer leur foi chrétienne. C'est à ces repas en commun, empreints d'amour fraternel, que se réfère le titre de ce recueil *Agape*. C'est pour moi un très grand plaisir de vous le présenter à l'occasion de la Dixième Assemblée de la FLM, organisée du 21 au 31 juillet 2003 à Winnipeg (Canada). L'Assemblée offre elle aussi à ses participant(e)s l'occasion de se rassembler autour d'une table pour manger, célébrer et partager leurs expériences d'amour et de guérison.

Le mot grec *agape* (littéralement «amour») s'applique à l'amour universel qui émane de Dieu. Il ne s'agit pas d'un terme abstrait. Au contraire, il évoque un mode de vie empreint de justice, de compassion, de respect mutuel, d'hospitalité, de service, de réconciliation et d'espérance. A l'origine, l'*agape* avait pour cadre la *koinonia*, la communauté des fidèles portée par l'amour de Dieu.

L'*agape* est indépendant du caractère «aimable» de la personne à laquelle il s'adresse. C'est un amour fondé sur le sacrifice et le don de soi. Il nous propose une modification radicale de nos rapports avec Dieu, avec soi-même, avec les autres et avec la nature. Il implique que nous changions notre manière de voir, de sentir et d'entendre. Les chants de ce recueil veulent susciter des manières différentes de voir, de se lamenter, de sentir, de célébrer et des formes d'expression nouvelles. L'amour ne s'exprime pas seulement par les mots sacrés de la sagesse ni par le langage des anges. Il est chuchoté, murmuré, crié dans la langue des pauvres, des défavorisé(e)s et des opprimé(e)s. Je suis convaincu que cette diversité d'expression est un élément fondamental de notre communion. C'est par ces formes de partage et d'échange que nous devenons réellement nous-mêmes. Ces chants de louange et de plainte venus du monde entier nous aident à nous réconcilier et à briser les barrières sociales, culturelles, économiques, de race et de sexe. Ils ne se contentent pas de parler de guérison, ils sont un facteur de guérison.

Ce recueil constitue une contribution luthérienne au mouvement œcuménique et liturgique. J'espère qu'après l'Assemblée, il sera utilisé dans toutes les rencontres luthériennes et œcuméniques, au niveau local et multiculturel. Ces chants ont été recueillis et choisis par des représentant(e)s des Églises membres de la FLM et des représentant(e)s des milieux œcuméniques*. Je voudrais remercier ce groupe, les nombreux consultant(e)s, ainsi que les Editions Oxford University Press, pour leur contribution à la vie de l'Assemblée.

* Júlio Cézar Adam, Joy Berg, Marc Chambron, Per Harling, Stephen Larson, Terry MacArthur, Simei Monteiro, Jimson Sanga, Scott Weidler, Dietrich Werner, Mabel Wu, Päivi Jussila (coordinatrice).

Prefacio

por el Rev. Dr. Ishmael Noko, Secretario General de la FLM

Los primeros cristianos y cristianas se congregaban alrededor de la mesa para comer, celebrar, dar testimonio, orar y fortalecerse en la fe cristiana. "Agape", título del presente cancionero, se refiere a estas comidas de comunión, a estas fiestas de amor. Con gran regocijo pongo en sus manos el presente libro, que queda a disposición en oportunidad de la Décima Asamblea de la FLM, la cual delibera en Winnipeg, Canadá, 21–31 de julio de 2003. La asamblea le ofrece a las personas participantes una oportunidad de reunirse alrededor de la mesa, a fin de comer, alabar y compartir sus experiencias de amor y sanación.

El término griego *agape* (literalmente, 'amor') describe el amor universal y omni-abarcador que fluye de Dios. No se trata de un concepto abstracto. Antes bien, se refiere a un modo de vida, caracterizado por la justicia, la compasión, el respeto mutuo, la hospitalidad, el servicio, la reconciliación y la esperanza. El lugar primordial donde se ubica el agape es la *koinonia*, la comunidad de los fieles, integrada por personas sustentadas por el amor de Dios.

El agape no se basa en la amabilidad de la persona amada. Antes bien, se trata de un amor basado en la abnegación y el altruismo. Presupone un cambio radical en la manera como la persona se relaciona con Dios, con las otras, consigo misma y con la naturaleza. Implica un cambio en la manera como la persona ve, gusta y oye. Los cantos contenidos en esta colección animan y promueven diversas formas y expresiones de ver, lamentarse, degustar y alabar. No solo se expresa el amor con palabras santas de sabiduría o en el lenguaje de los ángeles. También se susurra, se murmura y se clama en el lenguaje de los pobres, de los menesterosos y de los oprimidos. Considero que la variedad de expresiones resulta vital para nosotros en función de comunión. Al compartir e intercambiar de esta manera nos constituimos verdaderamente en lo que somos. Estas canciones de alabanza y de lamento, provenientes de todo el mundo, nos ayudan a reconciliar y derribar barreras sociales, culturales, de género y raciales. Esos cantos no solo se refieren a la sanación, sino que son sanación en sí mismos.

Este cancionero constituye una contribución luterana al movimiento ecuménico y litúrgico. Abrigo la esperanza de que, después de la asamblea, se utilice universalmente en reuniones luteranas y ecuménicas, como también en el ámbito multicultural local. Las canciones han sido escogidas y seleccionadas por un grupo de representantes de iglesias afiliadas a la FLM junto con representantes ecuménicos*. Deseo expresar mi agradecimiento a este grupo, a muchos otros especialistas y a la Oxford University Press por su contribución al devenir de la asamblea.

* Júlio Cézar Adam, Joy Berg, Marc Chambron, Per Harling, Stephen Larson, Terry MacArthur, Simei Monteiro, Jimson Sanga, Scott Weidler, Dietrich Werner, Mabel Wu, Päivi Jussila (coordinadora).

Notes on the Songs

Languages

- All songs are printed first in the original language, followed in some cases by another language spoken in the region, then translations—if they were available to us—in English, German, French, and Spanish.
- When a text is only a few words, it is printed in the original language only, and given non-singable translations.
- Non-singable translations are given in parentheses.
- Scripts other than Roman have been transliterated.

Music

- As far as possible, we have used original sources. Songs originating in the oral tradition tend to vary according to time and place, so we have published one version only.
- Some songs have been given optional instrumental lines. These are to suggest style, and it is expected that musicians will create their own instrumental parts to match their resources.
- Guitar chords have been given at pitch, so that keyboard players can improvise accompaniments. Keyboard accompaniments have been kept simple, and more accomplished players may wish to elaborate them.
- We have given original metronome markings where these were available. Metronome markings are to be taken as a guide; actual tempi will depend on factors such as acoustic, size of congregation, etc.
- The rhythmic impetus of songs from Africa and Latin America especially means that the singing of them is commonly accompanied by dance and other body movements.

Regional notes

The following notes will enable music leaders to capture the essence of the styles from the different regions.

Africa

- African songs are generally only accompanied by drums and other percussion instruments; South African songs are usually sung *a cappella*.
- Leader lines, and links between verses, tend to be improvised, and vary with each verse. What we have printed is a guide to common practice.

Asia

- Where no accompaniment or chord symbols are given, the most appropriate form of performance is unaccompanied, or with a solo instrument doubling the vocal line. Some songs, such as 'Yarabba ssalami', may be accompanied by oud or guitar playing the melody in repeated notes.

Latin America

- Dance rhythms are indicated and appropriate rhythmic patterns suggested. It is important to follow the rhythm and metronome markings.
- Regional instruments that commonly accompany the songs are listed. In the absence of these instruments, other equivalent instruments may be used. Percussion should be added only to those songs where indicated.
- A useful source of samba patterns is *http://www.channel1.com/users/jfrancis/UBB/patterns.htm*.

Europe and North America

- European and North American hymns, where shown in this book without guitar chords, should normally be sung with keyboard or unaccompanied.

Hinweise zu den Liedern

Sprachen

- Alle Lieder werden zunächst in ihrer Herkunftssprache wiedergegeben, in einigen Fällen folgt eine weitere in der Region gesprochene Sprache, dann folgen—wenn verfügbar—singbare Übersetzungen in Englisch, Deutsch, Französisch, und Spanisch.
- Wenn ein Text nur aus wenigen Worten besteht wird er nur in der Originalsprache wiedergegeben, ergänzt durch nicht-singbare Übersetzungen.
- Nicht-singbare Übersetzungen stehen in Klammern.
- Andere als die lateinischen Schrifttypen werden transkribiert.

Notensatz

- Soweit irgend möglich, haben wir die ursprünglichen musikalischen Quellen und Sätze verwandt. Lieder, die ihren Ursprung in der mündlichen Tradition haben, variieren bisweilen in der Melodie. In diesen Fällen haben wir nur eine Version wiedergegeben.
- Bei einigen Liedern haben wir Notensätze für optionale Instrumentalbegleitung hinzugefügt. Diese dienen lediglich dazu, den Stil der Begleitung anzudeuten. Musikalisch Talentierte können ihre eigenen Instrumentalversionen für die Begleitung der Lieder hinzufügen und sie auf ihre Möglichkeiten abstimmen.
- Begleitakkorde für die Gitarre sind in der Normalstimmung hinzugefügt, so dass auch auf dem Keyboard eine entsprechende Begleitung improvisiert werden kann. Begleithinweise für Keyboard sind einfach gehalten, fortgeschrittene Spieler können sie selbstverständlich anspruchsvoller ausarbeiten.
- Metronomangaben sind dem Notensatz hinzugefügt und entsprechen dem Original, wo die Angaben verfügbar waren. Sie sind als Hinweise zu verstehen, die aktuellen Tempi werden sicher auch nach Faktoren wie der akustischen Situation, Grösse der Gemeinde usw. zu gestalten sein.
- Der stärker rhythmisierte Charakter der Lieder aus Afrika und Lateinamerika ist dadurch bedingt, dass das Singen dieser Lieder zumeist durch gemeinsamen Tanz oder andere körperliche Bewegungen begleitet wird.

Hinweise zu den Herkunftsregionen

Die folgenden Hinweise sollen ChorleiterInnen und KirchenmusikerInnen befähigen, den wesentlichen Charakter der musikalischen Stile aus den verschiedenen Regionen genauer zu erfassen.

Afrika

- Lieder aus Afrika werden gewöhnlich nur durch Trommeln oder andere Rhythmusinstrumente begleitet; Lieder aus Südafrika werden zumeist *a cappella* gesungen.
- Melodien für VorsängerInnen und Verbindungsstücke zwischen einzelnen Versen werden häufig improvisiert und verändern sich von Vers zu Vers. Was wir abgedruckt haben ist als Hinweis auf die üblichste Praxis zu verstehen.

Asien

- Wo keine Begleitstimme oder Begleitakkorde angegeben sind, ist die gewöhnlichste Form der musikalischen Gestaltung diejenige ohne Begleitung – oder mit einem Soloinstrument, das die Vokalstimme verdoppelt. Einige Lieder, wie zum Beispiel ‚Yarabba ssalami‘, können durch eine Gitarre oder Oud, die die Melodie wiederholt spielt, begleitet werden.

Lateinamerika

- Angaben zu den Tanz- und Rhythmusstilen sind jeweils den Liedern hinzugefügt. Es ist wichtig, die Rhythmusangaben und Metronomangaben zu beachten.
- Traditionelle Instrumente aus der Region, mit denen die Lieder zumeist begleitet werden, sind genannt. Falls solche Instrumente vor Ort fehlen, können die Lieder mit ähnlichen Instrumenten begleitet werden. Schlagzeug sollte nur bei solchen Lieder hinzugefügt werden, wo es angezeigt ist.
- Eine hilfreiche Übersicht über die verschiedenen Samba-Tanzrhythmen findet sich im Internet unter: *http://www.channel1.com/users/jfrancis/UBB/patterns.htm*.

Europa und Nordamerika

- Lieder aus Europa oder Nordamerika, die ohne Begleitakkorde für Gitarre wiedergegeben werden, sollten normalerweise mit Keyboard oder Orgel-Begleitsatz oder ohne Begleitung gesungen werden.

Remarques sur les chants

Langues

- Tous les chants sont imprimés d'abord dans leur langue d'origine, suivie dans certains cas par une autre langue parlée dans la région, puis par la traduction – quand elle nous était disponible – en anglais, allemand, français et espagnol.
- Quand un texte n'a que quelques mots, il n'est imprimé que dans la langue originale, et l'on donne des traductions non chantables.
- Les traductions non chantables sont entre parenthèses.
- Les écritures non romaines ont été transcrites.

Musique

- Autant que possible, nous avons utilisé les sources d'origine. Les chants venant de la tradition orale ont tendance à changer selon les temps et les lieux, aussi ne publions-nous qu'une seule version.
- Certains chants comportent des lignes instrumentales facultatives qu'on peut ou non choisir. Ceci afin de suggérer un style, avec l'idée que les musicien(ne)s créeront leur propre version instrumentale, selon leurs possibilités.
- Des accords de guitare ont été indiqués pour que les joueurs de clavier puissent improviser les accompagnements. Ceux-ci sont volontairement simples, et des musicien(ne)s accompli(e)s pourront les enrichir.
- Nous avons donné les indications d'origine concernant le métronome quand celles-ci étaient disponibles. Ces indications pour le métronome ne sont qu'un guide, car les véritables tempi dépendront d'éléments tels que l'acoustique, la taille de la communauté, etc.
- L'élan rythmique des chants d'Afrique et d'Amérique Latine indique que ceux-ci sont souvent accompagnés de danses et autres mouvements corporels.

Remarques selon les régions

Les notes qui suivent aideront les dirigeant(e)s à prendre en compte les styles des différentes régions.

Afrique

- Les chants africains sont en général accompagnés seulement par des tambours et autres instruments à percussion; les chants sud-africains sont habituellement chantés *a cappella*.
- Les lignes directrices et les liaisons entre les strophes sont souvent improvisées, et varient avec chaque strophe. Ce que nous avons imprimé est un guide pour chanter en groupe.

Asie

- Lorsque ne sont indiqués ni accompagnement ni accords, il est conseillé d'interpréter sans accompagnement, ou avec un instrument solo doublant la ligne vocale. Certains chants, par exemple, «Yarabba ssalami», peuvent être accompagnés par un oud ou une guitare jouant la mélodie avec des notes répétées.

Amérique Latine

- Les rythmes de danse sont indiqués, et les modèles rythmiques qui conviennent sont suggérés. Il est important de suivre le rythme et les battements du métronome.
- Les instruments régionaux qui devraient normalement accompagner les chants sont indiqués. S'ils ne sont pas disponibles, d'autres instruments équivalents peuvent être utilisés. N'ajouter la percussion à ces chants que lorsque cela est indiqué.
- Une source utile de modèles de sambas est *http://www.channel1.com/users/jfrancis/UBB/patterns.htm*.

Europe et Amérique du Nord

- Les chants européens et nord-américains, quand ils sont dans ce livre sans accords de guitare, doivent être normalement chantés avec clavier, ou sans accompagnement.

Notas referentes a los cantos

Idiomas

- Todas las canciones figuran primero en su idioma original y luego, en algunos casos, en uno u otro idioma hablado en la región y, por fin, si disponíamos de traducciones, en inglés, alemán, francés y español.
- Cuando determinado texto consiste tan sólo de unas pocas palabras, lo hemos publicado solamente en su idioma original, con traducciones que no se prestan a ser cantadas.
- Las traducciones que no se prestan a ser cantadas, figuran entre paréntesis.
- Caligrafías que no son de letra romana han sido transliteradas en forma fonética.

Música

- En lo posible, hemos utilizado las fuentes originales. Canciones que tienen su origen en la tradición oral, pueden ofrecer diferentes variaciones según la época y el lugar de donde provienen, pero nos hemos limitado a tan sólo una versión.
- Algunas canciones figuran con indicaciones instrumentales facultativas para sugerir un estilo, lo que significa que los músicos podrán desarrollar sus propias melodías, según los recursos disponibles.
- Se indican los acordes de guitarra sobre el pentagrama, para que así los intérpretes al teclado puedan improvisar un acompañamiento. Los acordes de acompañamiento son más bien simples, y los intérpretes más experimentados podrán explayarse en el tema musical.
- Las indicaciones metronómicas disponibles figuran en esta obra como guía; el ritmo usado dependerá de factores tales como la acústica, el tamaño de la congregación, etc.
- El ímpetu rítmico de canciones de África y de América Latina sugiere que el canto es comúnmente acompañado de baile u otros movimientos del cuerpo.

Notas regionales

Con las siguientes notas tratamos de ayudar a los directores de música a captar lo esencial de los estilos de las diferentes regiones.

África

- Por lo general, las canciones africanas tan sólo llevan un acompañamiento de tambores y otros instrumentos de percusión; las canciones sudafricanas se suelen cantar sin acompañamiento instrumental.
- Hay cierta tendencia a improvisar la introducción y los enlaces entre las estrofas, que pueden variar para cada una de éstas. Lo que figura en esta publicación, es una guía para lo que comúnmente se practica.

Asia

- Cuando no hemos dado ni acompañamiento ni símbolo para los acordes, la representación más apropiada es sin acompañamiento, o con un instrumento único que duplica la voz humana. Algunas de las canciones, tales como 'Yarabba ssalami', pueden recibir un acompañamiento de oud (una especia de laúd del Oriente Medio) o guitarra repitiendo cada nota varias veces.

América Latina

- Hemos indicado los ritmos de baile y sugerido las formas rítmicas más apropiadas. Es importante seguir el ritmo y las indicaciones metronómicas.
- Hemos enumerado los instrumentos musicales que por lo general sirven de acompañamiento a las canciones publicadas. Si no se disponen de tales instrumentos, pueden usarse otros equivalentes. Tan sólo se deben usar instrumentos de percusión para las canciones en que lo hemos indicado.
- Para ritmos de samba sugerimos consultar el sitio Web: *http://www.channel1.com/users/ jfrancis/UBB/patterns.htm.*

Europa y América del Norte

- Los himnos europeos y norteamericanos que en esta publicación figuran sin acordes de guitarra, se deberán cantar por lo general con instrumentos de teclado o sin acompañamiento.

Agape

1 | A ivangeli ya famba

Trad. Xitswa, Mozambique

* insert names of countries or continents, e.g. India, America, Jamaica, UK, etc.

(The Gospel is going (is going) all over the world.
We will take it to *Africa, India, America, Jamaica, UK, etc.)

(Das Evangelium umrundet (umrundet) die Welt.
Wir bezeugen es in *Afrika, Indien, Amerika, Jamaica, UK, usw.)

(L'Evangile parcourt (parcourt) le monde.
Nous l'emmènerons en *Afrique, en Inde, en Amérique, en Jamaïque, au Royaume-Uni, etc.)

(El Evangelio va (va) por todo el mundo.
Lo llevaremos a *Africa, a India, a América, a Jamaica, al Reino Unido, etc.)

2 A ti, Señor, te pedimos (Confesión)

Ulises Torres

Trad., Chile

♩ = 80

A ti, Se - ñor, te pe - di - mos per -
A ti, Sen - hor, te pe - di - mos o
Have mer - cy, hear our con - fes - sion, O
Wir bit - ten dich, Gott, er - barm dich. Ver -
Par - don, Sei - gneur, pour nos fau - tes, pour

- dón en es - te mo - men - to por los pe - ca - dos de ac - cio -
teu per - dão, teu a - len - to; pe - ca - mos por nos - sos a -
God: blot out our mis - do - ings; for - give us where self - ish mo -
- gib, was wir vor dich brin - gen, was uns be - drückt und be - frem -
tous les pé - chés du mon - de, pour nos ac - tions mal - fai - san -

- nes, pa - la - bras y pen - sa - mien - tos.
- tos, pa - la - vras e pen - sa - men - tos.
- tives have scarred the earth we in - ha - bit.
- det, was Schat - ten wirft, was uns Angst macht.
- tes, pour nos pa - ro - les bles - san - tes.

Spanish

1 A ti, Señor, te pedimos
perdón en este momento
por los pecados de acciones,
palabras y pensamientos.

2 De tiempos inmemoriales
que nos hemos separado
de tu comunión bendita:
perdona nuestro pecado.

3 De tiempos inmemoriales
que nos hemos separado
de todos los que tú amas:
perdona nuestro pecado.

4 De tiempos inmemoriales,
en el alma del humano
hay luchas que lo destruyen:
perdona nuestro pecado.

Portuguese

1 A ti, Senhor, te pedimos
o teu perdão, teu alento;
pecamos por nossos atos,
palavras e pensamentos.

2 De tempos já sem memória
vivemos tão separados
da tua mesa bendita:
perdoa nossos pecados.

3 De tempos já sem memória
vivemos tão separados
de todos os que tu amas:
perdoa nossos pecados.

4 De tempos já sem memória
vivemos desesperados
em lutas, ódio e malícia:
perdoa nossos pecados.

tr. Jaci Maraschin

English

1 Have mercy, hear our confession,
O God: blot out our misdoings;
forgive us where selfish motives
have scarred the earth we inhabit.

2 Have mercy, hear our confession,
O God: forgive us the moments
when we have failed with compassion
to heal, encourage, enable.

3 Share out among us your Spirit,
that we may grow in awareness
and thus discern in each other
the human features of Jesus.

4 O God, you send us, forgiven,
into your world every morning
to speak, make peace among people:
each day a hopeful beginning!

tr. Fred Kaan

German

1 Wir bitten dich, Gott, erbarm dich.
Vergib, was wir vor dich bringen,
was uns bedrückt und befremdet,
was Schatten wirft, was uns Angst macht.

2 Wir bitten dich, Gott, vergib uns,
wir haben dich oft verraten.
Wir haben mit dir gebrochen
in Gedanken, Worten und Taten.

3 Wir bitten dich, Gott, vergib uns,
wir leben auf Kosten and'rer.
Weil wir nicht eins mit uns selbst sind,
fehlt uns der Atem zur Liebe.

4 Wir bitten dich, Gott, sei mit uns,
weil wir deine Nähe brauchen.
Wir bitten dich, Gott, bleib mit uns.
Zeig uns die Spuren des Friedens.

tr. Fritz Baltruweit

French

1 Pardon, Seigneur, pour nos fautes,
pour tous les péchés du monde,
pour nos actions malfaisantes,
pour nos paroles blessantes.

2 Depuis trop longtemps, nous sommes
loin de toi et de ta face,
sans communion, sans ta grâce.
Pardon, Seigneur, pour nos fautes.

3 Depuis trop longtemps, nos guerres
font mal à ton cœur de père,
nous qui sommes tes enfants.
Pardon, Seigneur, pour nos fautes.

4 Redonne-nous l'espérance,
et viens guérir nos souffrances,
et tous les péchés du monde.
Pardon, Seigneur, pour nos fautes.

tr. Marc Chambron

GUITAR

3

A Palavra do Senhor

based on Isaiah 55: 11 and Luke 19: 40

Unknown, South America

Canon

A Pa - la - vra do Se-nhor não lhe vol - ta - rá va - zi - a. A - mém,
La Pa - la - bra del Se - ñor__ no vuel-ve_a él va - cí - a. ¡A - mén,
Ne - ver will God's Word re-turn un-ful - filled and void of mean-ing, a - men,
Got-tes Wort kehrt nie-mals leer__ zu - rück, um-sonst ge-spro-chen. A - men,
La Pa - ro - le ne re-vient pas au Sei-gneur in - ac-com - plie. A - men,

a - mém! E se nós nos ca - lás - se - mos as pe-dras cla - ma - ri - am.
a - mén! Si no - so - tros ca - llá - ra - mos las pie-dras cla - ma - rí - an.
a - men! Were we si - lent, the ve - ry stones would shout a-loud, res-pond - ing:
a - men! Wenn wir schwei-gen, dann fan-gen selbst die Stei - ne an zu schrei - en.
a - men! Si nous de - meu - rons si - len-cieux, les pier-res ac - cla - me - ront.

A - mém, a - mém! A - - - mém, a - mém,
¡A - mén, a - mén! ¡A - - - mén, a - mén,
A - men, a - men! A - - - men, a - men,
A - men, a - men! A - - - men, a - men,
A - men, a - men! A - - - men, a - men,

a - mém, a - mém! A - - - mém, a - mém, a - mém!
a - mén, a - mén! ¡A - - - mén, a - mén, a - mén!
a - men, a - men! A - - - men, a - men, a - men!
a - men, a - men! A - - - men, a - men, a - men!
a - men, a - men! A - - - men, a - men, a - men!

English tr. Fred Kaan; German tr. Dieter Trautwein; French tr. Béatrice Bengtsson

4 Agios o Theos

From the Orthodox Liturgy, Greece

Byzantine chant,
Petros Lampadarios

A - gi - os o The - os, a - gi - os i - schy - ros,

a - gi - os a - tha - na - tos, e - le - i - son i - mas._____

(Holy God, Holy Mighty, Holy Immortal: have mercy on us.)

(Heiliger Gott, heiliger Mächtiger, heiliger Unsterblicher, erbarme dich unser.)

(Dieu saint, saint et fort, saint et immortel, aie pitié de nous.)

(Santo Dios, Santo Poderoso, Santo Immortal ¡à ten misericordia de nosotros!)

The key signature indicates that the note A is sung approximately a quarter tone flat.
The G drone should be sung on a neutral vowel.

5 | Aleluya Y'in Oluwa

Trad. Yoruba, Nigeria

Yoruba

1 Aleluya Y'in Oluwa.
Aleluya Y'in Oluwa.
O seun, o seun, o seun, o seun baba
Aleluya Y'in Oluwa.

2 E k'orin ayo s'Oluwa.
E k'orin ayo s'Oluwa.
ka f'ope fun ka si tun maa jo
e k'orin ayo s'Oluwa.

3 E k'orin e lu'lu f'Oluwa.
E k'orin e lu'lu f'Oluwa.
O seun, o seun, o seun, o seun baba
e k'orin e lu'lu f'Oluwa.

English

1 Alleluia, praise the Lord.
Alleluia, praise the Lord.
Praises, high praises, now bring to the Lord.
Alleluia, praise the Lord.

2 Songs of joy sing to the Lord.
Songs of joy sing to the Lord.
Dancing and singing your praises to God.
Songs of joy sing to the Lord.

3 Beat the drums; sing out for the Lord.
Beat the drums; sing out for the Lord.
Praises, high praises, give thanks to the Lord.
Beat the drums; sing out for the Lord.

tr. Emmanuel Badejo

German

1 Freudenlieder singt unserm Gott.
Freudenlieder singt unserm Gott.
Tanzt euren, singt euren Lobpreis zu Gott.
Freudenlieder singt unserm Gott.

2 Schlagt die Trommel, singt laut zu Gott.
Schlagt die Trommel, singt laut zu Gott.
Stampfender Trommelklang preist unsern Gott.
Schlagt die Trommel, singt laut zu Gott.

3 Halleluja, preist unsern Gott.
Halleluja, preist unsern Gott.
Leichtigkeit, Heiterkeit, preist unsern Gott.
Halleluja, preist unsern Gott.

tr. Horst Bracks

6a

All people that on earth do dwell

William Kethe
based on Psalm 100

88 88 (LM)
Melody by (or adapt.) Louis Bourgeois
harm. Claude Goudimel

All peo - ple that on earth do dwell, sing to the Lord with cheer - ful voice;
Nun jauchzt dem Her - ren, al - le Welt. Kommt her, zu sei - nem Dienst euch stellt;
Vous, qui sur la terre ha - bi - tez, chan - tez à plei - ne voix, chan - tez,
Oh pueb - los to - dos a - la - bad en al - ta voz a Dios can - tad,

him serve with fear, his praise forth tell. Come ye be - fore him and re - joice.
kommt mit Froh - lo - cken, säu - met nicht, kommt vor sein hei - lig An - ge - sicht.
ré - jou - is - sez-vous au Sei-gneur, é - ga - yez-vous à son hon - neur.
re - go - ci - ja - os en su ho-nor ser - vid a - le - gres al Se - ñor.

English

1 All people that on earth do dwell,
  sing to the Lord with cheerful voice;
  him serve with fear, his praise forth tell.
  Come ye before him and rejoice.

2 The Lord ye know is God indeed;
  without our aid he did us make;
  we are his folk, he doth us feed,
  and for his sheep he doth us take.

3 O enter then his gates with praise;
  approach with joy his courts unto;
  praise, laud, and bless his name always,
  for it is seemly so to do.

4 For why? The Lord our God is good;
  his mercy is for ever sure;
  his truth at all times firmly stood,
  and shall from age to age endure.

German

1 Nun jauchzt dem Herren, alle Welt.
  Kommt her, zu seinem Dienst euch stellt;
  kommt mit Frohlocken, säumet nicht,
  kommt vor sein heilig Angesicht.

2 Erkennt, dass Gott ist unser Herr,
  der uns erschaffen ihm zur Ehr.
  Als guter Hirt ist er bereit,
  zu führen uns auf gute Weid.

3 Die ihr nun wollet bei ihm sein,
  kommt, geht zu seinen Toren ein
  mit Loben durch der Psalmen Klang,
  zu seinem Hause mit Gesang.

4 Er ist voll Güt und Freundlichkeit,
  voll Lieb und Treu zu jeder Zeit.
  Sein Gnad währt immer dort und hier
  und seine Wahrheit für und für.

after Cornelius Becker

French

1 Vous, qui sur la terre habitez,
chantez à pleine voix, chantez,
réjouissez-vous au Seigneur,
égayez-vous à son honneur.

2 Lui seul est notre souverain,
c'est lui qui nous fit de sa main:
nous le peuple qu'il mènera,
le troupeau qu'il rassemblera.

3 Présentez-vous tous devant lui,
dans sa maison dès aujourd'hui;
célébrez son nom glorieux,
exaltez-le jusques aux cieux.

4 Pour toi, Seigneur, que notre amour
se renouvelle chaque jour:
ta bonté, ta fidélité,
demeurent pour l'éternité.

Roger Chapal,
after Théodore de Bèze

Spanish

1 Oh pueblos todos alabad
en alta voz a Dios cantad,
regocijaos en su honor
servid alegres al Señor.

2 El soberano Creador
de nuestra vida es el autor;
el pueblo suyo somos ya,
rebaño que el pastoreará.

3 A su santuario pues entrad,
y vuestras vidas ofrendad;
al nombre augusto dad loor,
que al mundo llena de esplendor.

4 Incomparable es su bondad,
y para siempre su verdad;
de bienes colma nuestro ser
su gracia no ha de fenecer.

tr. Federico J. Pagura

6b | Be present at our table, Lord (Table graces)

English

Be present at our table, Lord;
be here and everywhere adored.
This food now bless, and grant that we
may strengthened for your service be.

John Cennick (altd.)

German

1 Herr, gib uns unser täglich Brot.
Lass uns bereit sein, in der Not
zu teilen, was du uns gewährt.
Dein ist die Erde, die uns nährt.

2 Herr, du bist unser täglich Brot.
Du teilst dich aus in deinem Tod.
Wir loben dich und danken dir.
Aus deiner Liebe leben wir.

Edwin Nievergelt

French

A notre table, viens, Seigneur,
Nous t'adorons d'un même cœur.
Que tous les humains soient bénis
pour te fêter en Paradis.

tr. Marc Chambron

Spanish

A nuestra mesa ven, Señor
Te recibimos con amor.
Bendice, ahora, nuestro pan
y de tu gracia haz nos vivir.

tr. Simei Monteiro

7 Alleluia

Orthodox Liturgy, Kiev, Ukraine

Al - le - lu - i - a, Al - le - lu - i - a,

Al - - - - le - lu - i - a.

8

asato maa sad gamaya

Trad. Sanskrit, India

In slow, free time

1st time LEADER, 2nd time ALL

a - sa - to   maa   sad   ga - ma - ya,
Lead me through   quest   to   what is   real,
Füh - re mich   durch   Su - che zum   Ziel.
Con - duis - moi   du   faux   vers le   vrai,
Llé - va - me,   Dios,   al   des - ti - no.

ta - ma - so   maa____   jyo - tir   ga - ma - ya,
from the dark   night____   guide me   to the   light.
In dunk - ler   Nacht____   lass Licht   mich se - hen.
de l'ob - scu - ri - té____   vers la   lu - miè - re,
Guí - a - me,   oh Dios,_   a la   cla - ra   luz.

mri - tyor_____   maa____   am - ri - tam____   ga - ma - ya.
From   death_____   take me_   to the   realms____   of   liv - ing.
Vom   Tod_____   führ mich   in das   Land____   des   Le - bens.
et de   no - tre   mort____   vers la   vie____   en - tiè - re.
De la   muer - te   con - dú - ce - me   a_____   la   vi - da.

English tr. Fred Kaan; German tr. Dietrich Werner; French tr. Marc Chambron; Spanish tr. Martin Junge

13

9

Bendice, Señor, nuestro pan

Unknown, Argentina

Ben - di - ce, Se - ñor, nues - tro pan, y da
Now bless, Lord, the bread you have giv'n and give
Gott, seg - ne___ uns un - ser Brot, und gib
Sei - gneur viens bé - nir no - tre pain, et___

pan a los que tien - en___ ham - bre__ y ham-bre de jus - ti-cia a los que tien - en
bread to this our world that is hun-gry; to those with bread give hun-ger for true jus-tice
al - len Brot, die hung - rig___ sind, und gib Hun - ger nach Ge - rech-tig-keit den Sat -
nour - ris tous ceux qui ont faim. Don-ne faim___ de jus - tice à ceux qui ont du

pan. Ben - di - ce, Se - ñor, nues - tro pan.
now! And bless, Lord, the bread that we share.
- ten. Gott, seg - ne___ uns un - ser Brot.
pain. Sei - gneur viens bé - nir no - tre pain.

English tr. Fred Kaan; German tr. Dieter Trautwein; French tr. Marc Chambron

Bwana awabariki

Trad. Swahili, Tanzania

English tr. unknown; German tr. Dietrich Werner; French tr. Marc Chambron

11

Bí, a Íosa, im chroíse

Anon.

Trad., Ireland
arr. Anthony F. Carver

Gaelic

1 Bí, a Íosa, im chroíse i gcuimhne gach uair,
   bí, a Íosa, im chroíse le haithrí go luath,
   bí, a Íosa, im chroíse le cumann go buan,
   ó, a Íosa, 'Dhé dhílis, ná scar thusa uaim.

2 'Sé, a Íosa mo ríse, mo chara is mo ghrá;
   'sé, a Íosa mo dhídean ar pheacaí is ar bhás;
   'sé, a Íosa mo aoibhneas, mo scáthán de ghnáth;
   is a Íosa, 'Dhé dhílis, ná scar uaim go brách.

3 Bí, a Íosa, go síoraí im chroí is im bhéal,
   bí, a Íosa, go síoraí im thuigse mar an gcéann',
   bí, a Íosa, go síoraí im mheabhair mar léann,
   's ó, a Íosa, 'Dhé dhílis, ná fág mé liom féin.

English

1 O Jesus, every moment be in my heart and mind;
   O Jesus, stir my heart with sorrow for my sins;
   O Jesus, fill my heart with never-failing love;
   O Jesus, sweet Master, never part from me.

2 O Jesus is my king, my friend, and my love;
   O Jesus is my shelter from sinning and from death;
   O Jesus, my gladness, my mirror all my days;
   O Jesus, my dearest Lord, never part from me.

3 O Jesus, be for ever in my heart and my mouth;
   O Jesus, be for ever in my thought and my prayer;
   O Jesus, be for ever in my quiet mind;
   O Jesus, my sweet Lord, do not leave me alone.
                                        tr. George Otto Simms

German

1 O Jesus, alle Zeiten sei du in meinem Herz.
   O Jesus, mit Reue lass mich sehen meine Sünd'.
   O Jesus, meinen Frieden in deiner Liebe find'.
   O Jesus, Herr und Bruder, an meiner Seite bleib fest.

2 O Jesus, mein König, mein Freund und mein Halt.
   O Jesus, der Schutz gibt vor Abgrund und Sünd'.
   O Jesus, meine Freude, meine Hoffnung, jeden Tag.
   O Jesus, Herr und Bruder, an meiner Seite bleib fest.

3 O Jesus, meine Worte, meine Sinne lenke du.
   O Jesus, meiner Seele, aufgewühlt, schenke Ruh.
   O Jesus, meinem Denken, meinem Beten, gebe Ziel.
   O Jesus, Herr und Bruder, an meiner Seite bleib fest.
                                        tr. Dietrich Werner

12 | Cantai ao Senhor

based on Psalm 98

Unknown, Brazil
arr. Simei Monteiro

Vals ♩. = 56

INSTRUMENT (ad lib.)

Em   B7

Can -
Can -
O
Singt
Chan -

- tai   ao   Se - nhor   um   cân - ti - co   no - vo,   can -
- tad   al   Se - ñor   un   cán - ti - co   nue - vo,   can -
sing   to   the   Lord,   O   sing God   a   new song,   O
Gott, un - serm Herrn,   singt ihm neu - e   Lie - der, singt
- tons au   Sei - gneur   un   nou - veau can - ti - que, chan -

Em   B7

No percussion is used in this song.

(verses overleaf)

Portuguese

1 Cantai ao Senhor um cântico novo,
cantai ao Senhor um cântico novo,
cantai ao Senhor um cântico novo,
cantai ao Senhor, cantai ao Senhor!

2 Porque ele fez, e faz maravilhas, (x3)
cantai ao Senhor, cantai ao Senhor!

3 Cantai ao Senhor, bendizei o seu nome. (x3)
Cantai ao Senhor, cantai ao Senhor!

4 É ele quem dá o Espírito Santo. (x3)
Cantai ao Senhor, cantai ao Senhor!

5 Jesus é o Senhor! Amén, aleluia! (x3)
Cantai ao Senhor, cantai ao Senhor!

Spanish

1 Cantad al Señor un cántico nuevo,
cantad al Señor un cántico nuevo,
cantad al Señor un cántico nuevo,
cantad al Señor, cantad al Señor.

2 Porque el creó, creó maravillas: (x3)
cantad al Señor, cantad al Señor.

3 La peña se abrió, y agua bebimos: (x3)
cantad al Señor, cantad al Señor.

4 El es quien nos da el Espíritu Santo: (x3)
cantad al Señor, cantad al Señor.

5 ¡Jesus es Señor! ¡Amén, aleluya! (x3)
Cantad al Señor, cantad al Señor.

English

1 O sing to the Lord, O sing God a new song.
O sing to the Lord, O sing God a new song.
O sing to the Lord, O sing God a new song.
O sing to our God, O sing to our God.

2 By this holy power our God has done wonders. (x3)
O sing to our God, O sing to our God.

3 So dance for our God and blow all the trumpets. (x3)
O sing to our God, O sing to our God.

4 O shout to our God, who gave us the Spirit. (x3)
O sing to our God, O sing to our God.

5 For Jesus is Lord! Amen, alleluia. (x3)
O sing to our God, O sing to our God.
tr. Gerhard Cartford

German

1 Singt Gott, unserm Herrn, singt ihm neue Lieder!
 Singt Gott, unserm Herrn, singt ihm neue Lieder!
 Singt Gott, unserm Herrn, singt ihm neue Lieder!
 Singt Gott, unserm Herrn, singt Gott, unserm Herrn!

2 Denn Wunder tat Gott, er tut sie noch immer. (x3)
 Singt Gott, unserm Herrn, singt Gott, unserm Herrn!

3 Jauchzt Gott, alle Welt, lobsingt seinem Namen! (x3)
 Singt Gott, unserm Herrn, singt Gott, unserm Herrn!

4 Gott gib uns den Geist, der aufweckt und sammelt! (x3)
 Singt Gott, unserm Herrn, singt Gott, unserm Herrn!

5 Denn Jesus ist der Herr. Amen, halleluja! (x3)
 Singt Gott, unserm Herrn, singt Gott, unserm Herrn!
 tr. Dorival Ristoff and Dieter Trautwein

French

1 Chantons au Seigneur un nouveau cantique.
 Chantons au Seigneur un nouveau cantique.
 Chantons au Seigneur un nouveau cantique.
 Chantons au Seigneur, chantons au Seigneur.

2 C'est lui, et lui seul qui fait des merveilles. (3x)
 Chantons au Seigneur, chantons au Seigneur.

3 Bénissez le nom du Seigneur du monde. (3x)
 Chantons au Seigneur, chantons au Seigneur.

4 Que le Saint-Esprit conduise la danse. (3x)
 Chantons au Seigneur, chantons au Seigneur.

5 Jésus est Seigneur, amen, alléluia. (3x)
 Chantons au Seigneur, chantons au Seigneur.
 tr. Marc Chambron

13 | Come, Holy Spirit, descend on us

Words and music by
the Wild Goose Worship Group, Scotland

Come, Ho - ly Spi - rit, de - scend on us, de -
Komm, Geist des Le - bens, komm ü - ber uns, komm
Viens, Es - prit Saint, viens, de - scend sur nous, de -

- scend on us. We ga - ther here in Je - - sus'
ü - ber uns, und un - ter uns wächst Got - - tes
- scend sur nous. Ras - sem - ble nous en Jé - - sus-

verses 1–7   verse 8

Come,__ Ho-ly Spi - rit.

name.(*hum*)_____   2. Come, Breath of   name._____
Reich._____   2. Komm, Brot des   Reich._____
- Christ._____   2. Viens, souf - fle   Christ._____

English

1 Come, Holy Spirit, descend on us,
      descend on us.
  We gather here in Jesus' name.

2 Come, Breath of Heaven, …

3 Come, Word of Mercy, …

4 Come, Fire of Judgement, …

5 Come, Great Creator, …

6 Come to unite us, …

7 Come to disturb us, …

8 Come to inspire us, …

German

1 Komm, Geist des Lebens, komm über uns,
      komm über uns,
  und unter uns wächst Gottes Reich.

2 Komm, Brot des Himmels, …

3 Komm, du Erbarmen, …

4 Komm, Flamme Gottes, …

5 Komm, grosser Schöpfer, …

6 Komm, zu versöhnen, …

7 Komm, störe uns auf, …

8 Komm, gehe uns auf, …
                    tr. Thomas Laubach

French

1 Viens, Esprit Saint, viens, descend sur nous,
      descend sur nous.
  Rassemble nous en Jésus-Christ.

2 Viens, souffle divin, …

3 Viens, verbe de grâce, …

4 Viens, feu du jugement, …

5 Viens, puissant créateur, …

6 Viens pour nous unir, …

7 Viens nous déranger, …

8 Viens nous inspirer, …
                    tr. Hans Schmocker

14 | Crashing waters at creation

Sylvia Dunstan

CRASHING WATERS 87 87
William A. Cross, Canada

Crash - ing____ wa - ters at cre - a - tion,
To - sen - de Was - ser, im Akt der____ Schöp - fung,

or - dered by the____ Spi - rit's breath, first to____ wit - ness
fin - den____ Ruh durch des Schöp - fers Kraft, Him - mel und Er - de,

day's be - gin - ning from the____ bright - ness of____ night's death.
A - bend und Mor - gen, wur - den____ durch des Schöp - fers Macht.

English

1 Crashing waters at creation,
 ordered by the Spirit's breath,
 first to witness day's beginning
 from the brightness of night's death.

2 Parting water stood and trembled
 as the captives passed on through,
 washing off the chains of bondage
 channel to a life made new.

3 Cleansing water once at Jordan
 closed around the one foretold,
 opened to reveal the glory
 ever new and ever old.

4 Living water, never ending,
 quench the thirst and flood the soul.
 Wellspring, Source of life eternal,
 drench our dryness, make us whole.

German

1 Tosende Wasser, im Akt der Schöpfung,
 finden Ruh durch des Schöpfers Kraft,
 Himmel und Erde, Abend und Morgen,
 wurden durch des Schöpfers Macht.

2 Wasser des Schilfmeers standen zur Seite,
 Israels Durchzug zu bereiten.
 Ketten der Knechtschaft, aufzubrechen,
 Wege zur Freiheit öffnen stets neu.

3 Wasser des Jordans, im Bad der Taufe,
 umschlossen den, der ist Gottes Sohn,
 er, Gottes Zeichen, Träger des Geistes,
 Gottes Lieb' er zeiget schon.

4 Wasser des Lebens, fliesst ohne Ende,
 still uns'ren Durst und erfrisch uns all,
 Quell ew'gen Lebens, Weltenwende,
 erfüll die Schöpfung, mach uns heil.
 tr. Dietrich Werner

15 Chimwemwe mwa Yesu

Trad. Nyanja, Zambia

♩ = 120

LEADER ... ALL

1. Chi - mwe - mwe mwa Ye - su, chi - mwe - mwe mwa Ye - su, chi -
2. U - mo - zi mwa Ye - su, u - mo - zi mwa Ye - su, u -
3. Mu - te - nde mwa Ye - su, mu - te - nde mwa Ye - su, mu -

LEADER ALL

- mwe - mwe mwa Ye - su, chi - mwe - mwe mwa Ye - su, chi - mwe - mwe mwa Ye - su, chi -
- mo - zi mwa Ye - su, u - mo - zi mwa Ye - su, u - mo - zi mwa Ye - su, u -
- te - nde mwa Ye - su, mu - te - nde mwa Ye - su, mu - te - nde mwa Ye - su, mu -

LEADER ALL

- mwe - mwe mwa Ye - su, chi - mwe - mwe mwa Ye - su.
- mo - zi mwa Ye - su, u - mo - zi mwa Ye - su.
- te - nde mwa Ye - su, mu - te - nde mwa Ye - su.

(1. Rejoice in Jesus. 2. We're one in Jesus. 3. Peace in Jesus.)

(1. Freut euch an Jesus. 2. Wir sind einig in Jesus. 3. Friede in Jesus.)

(1. Réjouissez-vous en Jésus. 2. Nous sommes un en Jésus. 3. Paix en Jésus.)

(1. Regocijémonos en Jesús. 2. Somos uno en Jesús. 3. Paz en Jesús.)

16

Du är helig

Words and music by
Per Harling, Sweden

som___ kom - mer hit just nu,___ Väl___
Bless - ed are you com-ing here___ to your
kommst in dei - nes Vol-kes Zelt,___ kommst zu
en nos â - mes ton la - bour.___ Pour ton
te a - do - ra - mos con fer - vor.___ A tu i -

sig - nan-de vår jord,___ blir till bröd på vår jord._
church in wine and bread,_ raised from soil, raised from dead.
uns in Wein und Brot,_ bringst uns Le - ben statt Tod._
peuple le pain, le vin___ de la terre ca-deau di-vin._
- gle - sia en vi - no y pan___ nue - va vi - da a - sí le das._

Part 2

Du är he - lig,___ du är hel - het,___
You are ho - ly,___ you are whole - ness,___
Du bist hei - lig,___ Le - bens - fül - le,___
Tu es saint,___ plé - ni - tu - de,___
E - res san - to,___ e - res Dios,___

English tr. Per Harling; German tr. Wolfgang Leyk (altd.); French tr. Joëlle Gouël; Spanish tr. Rachel Achon

1 och 2 kan sjungas samtidigt.
Parts 1 and 2 can be sung at the same time.
Teile 1 und 2 können gleichzeitig gesungen werden.
Les deux parties peuvent se chanter en même temps.
Las partes 1 y 2 se pueden cantar al mismo tiempo.

17 Du satte dig selv i de nederstes sted

Words and music by
Merete Wendler, Denmark

Du sat - te dig selv i de ne - der-stes sted.__ Du sat - te dig
You came, took your place with the hum-ble and poor.__ You came and took
Du hast dich ge - stellt zu den Ar-men am Rande.__ Du hast an - ge -

op mod de sto-res for - træd.__ Du sat - te dig ind i de y - der-stes nød.
is - sue with sta-tus and power.__ You came and de - scend - ed to depths of des-pair.
- fragt die vom ho - hen Stande. Du hast dich ver - letz - lich ge-macht bis zum Tod.

__ Du sat - te dig ud o - ver døds-angst og død.__
__ You faced death and dy - ing-its hor - ror and scare.__
__ Du hast__ ge - tragen al - ler Men - schen Not.__

30

Danish

1 Du satte dig selv i de nederstes sted.
Du satte dig op mod de stores fortræd.
Du satte dig ind i de yderstes nød.
Du satte dig ud over dødsangst og død.

2 Nu taler du til os fra højeste sted,
hvor ingen kan udsätte dig for fortræd,
og lever og lider dog med os endnu,
så ingen er mere i live end du.

3 Du kæmper i verden for frihed og fred.
Når andre gir op, blir du viljefast ved.
Du følger os ind i den yderste nød,
og kalder os ud af den inderste død.

4 Du sender os ned i de nederstes sted.
Du sätter os op mod de stores fortræd.
Du lever i os i de inderste lag.
Vi lever i dig på den yderste dag.

English

1 You came, took your place with the humble and poor.
You came and took issue with status and power.
You came and descended to depths of despair.
You faced death and dying—its horror and scare.

2 Today you are with us in 'words from great height',
where nothing can stifle the reach of your light;
you stay with your people in sickness and health,
thus none is more truly alive than your Self.

3 You share the world's struggle for freedom and peace,
and never give up until all are released.
You follow us into the depths of despair
and raise us to life from what death would ensnare.

4 You send us to sit with the humble and poor,
and—with them—rise up against wielders of power.
You, deep in our being, bring hope to our hearts;
in you we're alive until earth-light departs.
tr. Fred Kaan

German

1 Du hast dich gestellt zu den Armen am Rande.
Du hast angefragt die vom hohen Stande.
Du hast dich verletzlich gemacht bis zum Tod.
Du hast getragen aller Menschen Not.

2 Du bist uns nah, wenn wir nah sind den Armen.
Wo's dunkel ist, kann doch dein Licht nicht ersticken.
Ob Krankheit drückt, Schmerz oder Sterben sich anschickt,
lebendig wirkst du als uns're heilende Kraft.

3 Du gibst nicht auf, bis alle Welt findet Frieden.
Du lässt nicht nach, bis wer gefangen ist frei.
Du lässt uns in tiefster Not nicht allein,
willst Retter uns und aller Heiland sein.

4 Du sendest uns zu Orten, wo Menschen leiden,
den Aufstand zu proben, neues Leben bereiten.
Tief in uns schaffst Du selbst unsere Hoffnung.
In dir wir leben bis zu unserem End.
tr. Dietrich Werner

18

Dvasia Šventoji, ateiki

Veni Sancte Spiritus
tr. M. Mažvydas

Trad., Lithuania
arr. Rimantas Sliužinskas

Dva - sia Šven - to - ji, a - tei - ki ir
O ho - ly, lov - ing Spi - rit, come, give
Komm Heil' - ger Geist, ent - zün - de uns, lass

iš dan - gaus mums nu - švies - ki, švie -
sight to blind and voice to dumb, give
sehn die Blin - den, öffne den Mund, die

- sy - bės sa - vo spin - du - lį! A -
hope, so we may not suc - cumb. Al -
Hoff - nung lass nicht un - ter - gehn. Hal -

- le - liu - ja! A - le - liu - ja!
- le - lu - ia! Al - le - lu - ia!
- le - lu - ja! Hal - le - lu - ja!

Lithuanian

1 Dvasia Šventoji, ateiki
ir iš dangaus mums nušvieski,
šviesybės savo spindulį!
Aleliuja! Aleliuja!

2 Ateik, ak Tėve vargdienių.
Ateik, davėja dovanų!
Ateik, šviesybe širdelių!
Aleliuja! Aleliuja!

3 Linksmintoja geriausioji,
viešnia laukta širdžių esi,
saldų darai mums atvėsį.
Aleliuja! Aleliuja!

4 Tu darbuose pailsini,
o troškume atvėsini,
ir verkiantį palinksmini!
Aleliuja! Aleliuja!

English

1 O holy, loving Spirit, come,
give sight to blind and voice to dumb,
give hope, so we may not succumb.
Alleluia! Alleluia!

2 Come, God of gifts, empower us,
come, Light of Light, enlighten us,
come, God of truth, deliver us.
Alleluia! Alleluia!

3 O Spirit, fire, wind and dove,
give light to all from heav'n above,
give every longing heart your love.
Alleluia! Alleluia!

4 O Spirit, purify our soul,
come, healing wind, and make us whole,
give joy, give faith and be our goal.
Alleluia! Alleluia!

tr. Per Harling

German

1 Komm Heil'ger Geist, entzünde uns,
lass sehn die Blinden, öffne den Mund,
die Hoffnung lass nicht untergehn.
Halleluja! Halleluja!

2 Komm Heil'ger Geist, belebe uns,
die Gaben des Geistes, die schenke uns,
zur Wahrheit du berufe uns.
Halleluja! Halleluja!

3 Komm Heil'ger Geist, verwandle uns.
Geist, Feuer und Wind vermehr geschwind,
mit deiner Lieb rühr jeden an.
Halleluja! Halleluja!

4 Komm Heil'ger Geist, und mach uns heil.
Versöhne uns in aller Welt.
Versöhnte Kirche lass uns sein.
Halleluja! Halleluja!

tr. Dietrich Werner

19

Du bist unser alles

St Columbanus

Sr. Adelheid Wenzelmann, Germany

Du	bist	un -	ser	al -	les,	un -	ser
Source	of	all	our	be -	ing,	fount	of
Tu	es	tout	pour	nous,	toi,	no -	tre
Tu	lo	e -	res	to -	do,	nues -	tra

Le -	ben,	un -	ser	Licht,	un -	ser	Heil,
liv -	ing,	you	are	light,	heal -	ing	power!
vie,	et	no -	tre	jour,	no -	tre	pain
vi -	da,	nues -	tra	luz,	la	sa -	lud,

un -	se -	re	Spei -	se,	un -	ser	Trank,
Bread	we	are	break -	ing,	wine	we	share,
et	no -	tre	sa -	lut,	no -	tre	source,
nues -	tro a -	li -	men -	to,	el	a -	gua,

un -	ser	Gott.
speak	your	Name!
no -	tre	Dieu.
nues -	tro	Dios.

English tr. Fred Kaan; French tr. Marc Chambron; Spanish tr. Martin Junge

20 | Eat this bread

based on John 6: 47–58

Jacques Berthier
for the Taizé Community, France

♩ = 80

Eat this bread, drink this cup, come to me and nev - er be hun - gry.
Prends ce pain, bois ce vin, viens à moi, et tu n'au - ras plus faim.
Esst das Brot, trinkt den Wein, kommt zu mir, seid nim-mer-mehr hun - grig!

G   C   Am   D   Bm   Em   Dsus   D

Eat this bread, drink this cup, trust in me and you will not thirst.
Manges et bois, crois en moi, et ma paix se - ra a - vec toi.
Esst das Brot, trinkt den Wein, glaubt an mich, seid nim-mer-mehr durstig!

G   D   Em   Bm   C   Dsus   D   G

(Come este pan, bebe esta copa, ven a mi y no tengas nunca hambre. Come este pan, bebe esta copa, confía en mi y no pasarás sed.)

May be sung as ostinato, or alternating with the verses on the next page.

36

37

21 | E toru nga mea

based on 1 Corinthians 13: 13

Maori, Aotearoa New Zealand

LEADER

E to - ru nga mea _____ Nga mea nu
Of all things that are _____ three mat - ter
Nun a - ber bleiben _____ drei teu - re

ALL

E to - ru nga mea
Of all things that are
Nun a - ber bleiben

nui _____ E kii a - na _____ Te Pai - pe -
most. _____ They are des - cribed _____ in Ho - ly
Worte _____ der Bi - bel, Worte _____ für uns ge -

Nga mea nu nui E kii a - na
three mat - ter most. They are des-cribed
drei teu - re Worte der Bi - bel, Worte

- ra _____ Wha - ka - po - no _____ Tu-ma - na -
Writ: _____ the first of them: faith! _____ the se - cond:
- geben: _____ Glaub', Hoff-nung und Liebe, _____ a - ber die

Te Pai - pe - ra Wha - ka - po - no
in Ho - ly Writ: the first of them: faith!
für uns ge-geben: Glaub', Hoff-nung und Liebe,

- ko_____ Ko te mea nui_____ Ko te A - ro - ha._____
hope!_____ the third, the best,_____ the prac-tice of love!____
Liebe,_____ a - ber die Liebe,_____ bleibt im-mer die grösste.__

Tu-ma - na - ko   Ko te mea nui   Ko te A - ro - ha._____
the se-cond: hope!   the third, the best,   the prac-tice of love!____
a - ber die Liebe,   a - ber die Liebe, bleibt im-mer die grösste.__

English tr. Fred Kaan; German tr. Dietrich Werner

(Il y a trois choses essentielles. C'est ce que disent les mots vivants de la Bible: la foi, l'espérance, mais la plus grande, c'est l'amour.)

(Tres palabras son valiosas, la Biblia las mantiene vivas. Una es la fe, la otra esperanza. Pero la mayor de ellas es amor.)

22

El cielo canta alegría

Words and music by
Pablo Sosa, Argentina

Carnavalito ♩ = 102

Cm ... Ab Bb Eb

El cie - lo can - ta a - le - grí - a, ¡A - le - lu - ya!
Hea - ven is sing - ing for joy,___ Al - le - lu - ia!
Him - mel er - klin - gen vor Freu - de, Hal - le - lu - ja!

Cm ... G7 ... Cm

por - que en tu vi - da y la mí - a bri - lla la glo - ria de Dios.
for in your life and in mine is shin - ing the glo - ry of God.
Denn dein und mein Le - ben glän - zen im_ Licht, das Gott rühmt und ehrt.

Bb ... Eb ... Bb7 ... Eb

¡A - le - lu - ya! ¡A - le - lu - ya!
Al - le - lu - ia! Al - le - lu - ia!
Hal - le - lu - ja! Hal - le - lu - ja!

Bb ... Eb ... Ab Gm Cm

¡A - le - lu - ya! ¡A - le - lu - ya!
Al - le - lu - ia! Al - le - lu - ia!
Hal - le - lu - ja! Hal - le - lu - ja!

Carnavalito

SHAKERS

CONGAS

GUITARS ... *sim.*

BASS

Instruments: charango and quenas (or guitar and recorder/flute)

Spanish

1 El cielo canta_alegría, ¡Aleluya!
porque_en tu vida_y la mía brilla la gloria de Dios.
¡Aleluya! ¡Aleluya! ¡Aleluya! ¡Aleluya!

2 El cielo canta_alegría, ¡Aleluya!
porque_a tu vida_y la mía las une_el amor de Dios.

3 El cielo canta_alegría, ¡Aleluya!
porque tu vida_y la mía proclamarán al Señor.

English

1 Heaven is singing for joy, Alleluia!
for in your life and in mine is shining the glory of God.
Alleluia! Alleluia! Alleluia! Alleluia!

2 Heaven is singing for joy, Alleluia!
for your life and mine unite in the love of the Lord.

3 Heaven is singing for joy, Alleluia!
for your life and mine will always bear witness to God.
tr. Pablo Sosa

German

1 Himmel erklingen vor Freude, Halleluja!
Denn dein und mein Leben glänzen im Licht, das Gott rühmt und ehrt.
Halleluja! Halleluja! Halleluja! Halleluja!

2 Himmel erklingen vor Freude, Halleluja!
Denn dein und mein Leben sind durch die Liebe Gottes vereint.

3 Himmel erklingen vor Freude, Halleluja!
Denn dein und mein Leben können ein Zeugnis geben für Gott.
tr. Dieter Trautwein

23

Fader vår

Matthew 6: 9–13

Egil Hovland, Norway

Fa-der vår, du som er i him-mel-en. La ditt navn hol-des hel - lig.
Our Fa - ther in hea - ven, hal-lowed be your_ name, your
Va - ter un - ser im Him - mel. Hei - lig sei dein_ Na - me.

La ditt ri - ke kom - me.__ La din vil - je skje på jor-den som i
king - dom_ come, your_ will_ be__ done on earth_ as in
Dein_ Reich kom - me. Dein Wil - le ge - scheh auf Er-den wie im

him-mel-en. Gi oss i dag vårt dag - li - ge brød. For - lat oss vår skyld, som
hea - ven. Give us to - day our dai - ly___ bread. For - give us our sins as
Him - mel. Gib heu-te un - ser täg - li-ches Brot. Ver - gib uns'-re Schuld, wie

vi___ og for - la - ter vå - re skyld-ne - re. Led oss ik - ke inn i___
we for - give___ those who sin a - gainst us. Lead us not in - to temp -
wir___ ver - ge - ben uns'-ren Schul-di-gern. Füh - re uns nicht in Ver -

fris - tel - se, men frels oss fra det on - de.   For___ ri - ket er
-ta - tion but de - li - ver us from e - vil.   For the king - dom, the
-su - chung, er - lös uns von dem Bö - sen.   Denn das Reich und die

ditt, og___ mak - ten og æ - ren nå og i e - vig - het. A - men.
power and the glo - ry are yours_ now and for e - ver. A - men.
Kraft und die Herr-lich-keit sind dein_ jetzt und in E - wig - keit. A - men.

For God alone

Words and music by
Eleanor Daley, Canada

For_ God a - lone my_ soul a - waits in si - - - - lence.
Auf_ Gott al - lein harrt mei - ne See - le, stil - - - - le.
C'est Dieu seul_ que mon âme at - tend en si - - len - ce.
Mi_ al - ma es - pe - ra_ so - lo a Dios en si - - len - cio.

German tr. Dorothea Wulfhorst; French tr. Marc Chambron; Spanish tr. Martin Junge

For the healing of the nations

Fred Kaan, Netherlands/England

WESTMINSTER ABBEY 87 87 87
Henry Purcell, England

For the heal - ing__ of the na - tions, God, we pray__ with
Für die Hei - lung al - ler Völ - ker__ bit - ten wir__ mit
Veuil - le gué - rir__ tous les peu - ples, O Sei - gneur,__ nous

one__ ac - cord; for a just and__ e - qual shar - ing
ei - nem__ Mund um ge - rech - tes,__ glei - ches Tei - len
t'en pri - ons; ap - prends - nous le__ vrai__ par - ta - ge

of__ the__ things__ that earth af - fords. To a life of
auf__ dem glei - chen Er - den - rund. Hilf, dass wir in
des__ biens de__ ta cré - a - tion. Et que ton a -

love in ac - tion help us rise and pledge__ our__ word.
tät' - ger Lie - be wu - chern mit dem eig - nen__ Pfund.
- mour in - spi - re nos pa - roles et nos__ ac - tions.

English

1 For the healing of the nations,
  God, we pray with one accord;
  for a just and equal sharing
  of the things that earth affords.
  To a life of love in action
  help us rise and pledge our word.

2 Lead us forward into freedom,
  from despair your world release;
  that, redeemed from war and hatred,
  all may come and go in peace.
  Show us how through care and goodness
  fear will die and hope increase.

3 All that kills abundant living,
  let it from the earth be banned:
  pride of status, race or schooling,
  dogmas that obscure your plan.
  In our common quest for justice
  may we hallow life's brief span.

4 You, Creator God, have written
  your great name on humankind;
  for our growing in your likeness
  bring the life of Christ to mind;
  that by our response and service
  earth its destiny may find.

German

1 Für die Heilung aller Völker
  bitten wir mit einem Mund
  um gerechtes, gleiches Teilen
  auf dem gleichen Erdenrund.
  Hilf, dass wir in tät'ger Liebe
  wuchern mit dem eignen Pfund.

2 Führ uns, Vater, in die Freiheit,
  mach uns von Verzweiflung frei,
  dass erlöst von Hass und Kriegen
  Friede mit uns allen sei.
  Zeig uns, wie durch Hilf und Güte
  Angst stirbt, Hoffnung wächst herbei.

3 Alles, was das Leben tötet,
  stelle unter deinen Bann:
  Stolz auf Stellung, Farbe, Klasse,
  Lehren gegen deinen Plan.
  Noch im Kampf für das, was recht ist,
  sehn wir Leben heilig an.

4 Schöpfer, du schreibst deinen Namen
  tief ins Buch der Menschheit ein;
  lass in uns dein Bildnis wachsen,
  hilf uns, Christus näher sein,
  dass durch uns'res Lebens Antwort
  Erde glänzt in deinem Schein.
  tr. Dieter Trautwein

French

1 Veuille guérir tous les peuples,
  O Seigneur, nous t'en prions;
  apprends-nous le vrai partage
  des biens de ta création.
  Et que ton amour inspire
  nos paroles et nos actions.

2 Conduis-nous, conduis le monde,
  vers la joie, la liberté;
  sans les haines, sans les guerres,
  que tous puissent vivre en paix.
  Aide-nous à mieux répandre
  l'espérance et la bonté.

3 Que la vie reste première,
  que soit banni ce qui tue;
  que l'orgueil, la suffisance,
  l'argent ne dominent plus.
  Que la justice progresse,
  qu'elle soit partout vécue.

4 Ton nom, Seigneur, d'âge en âge,
  est inscrit sur les humains;
  tous, créés à ton image,
  c'est le Christ qui nous fait tiens.
  Que, par notre obéissance,
  le monde aille à son destin.
  tr. Marc Chambron

26 | Gloria a Dios

Unknown, Peru

Andean instruments: charango, zamponãs, quenas, percussion

Spanish

1 Gloria a Dios, gloria a Dios, gloria en los cielos.
   A Dios la gloria por siempre.
   Aleluya, amen. Aleluya, amen. Aleluya, amen.

2 Gloria a Dios, gloria a Dios, gloria a Jesucristo.

3 Gloria a Dios, gloria a Dios, gloria al Espíritu Santo.

English

1 Glory to God, glory to God, glory in the highest.
   To God be glory forever.
   Alleluia, amen. Alleluia, amen. Alleluia, amen.

2 Glory to God, glory to God, glory to Christ Jesus.

3 Glory to God, glory to God, glory to the Spirit.

German

1 Ehre sei Gott, Ehre sei Gott, Ehre in der Höhe.
   Gebt Gott die Ehre für immer.
   Halleluja, amen. Halleluja, amen. Halleluja, amen.

2 Ehre sei Gott, Ehre sei Gott, Ehr' sei Jesus Christus.

3 Ehre sei Gott, Ehre sei Gott, Ehr' dem Heil'gen Geiste.
   tr. Dieter Trautwein

French

1 Gloire à Dieu, gloire à Dieu, à Dieu, gloire dans les hauts lieux.
   Gloire au Seigneur, gloire à jamais.
   Alléluia, amen. Alléluia, amen. Alléluia, amen.

2 Gloire à Dieu, gloire à Dieu, à Dieu, gloire au Seigneur Jésus.

3 Gloire à Dieu, gloire à Dieu, à Dieu, gloire à l'Esprit très saint.
   tr. Joëlle Gouël

27 | Gloria in excelsis Deo!

Luke 2: 14

GLORIA III
Jacques Berthier
for the Taizé Community, France

Canon

$\downarrow$. = 126

(Glory to God in the highest!)

(Ehre sei Gott in der Höhe!)

(Gloire à Dieu dans les lieux très-hauts!)

(¡Gloria a Dios en las alturas!)

Gospodi pomilui

from the Orthodox Liturgy, Ukraine

Gos - po-di po - mi - lui, Gos - po-di po - mi - lui,

Gos - po-di po - mi - - - - lui.

(Lord, have mercy.)

(Herr, erbarme dich.)

(Seigneur, aie pitié de nous.)

(Señor, ten piedad.)

May be sung by three-part women's or three-part men's voices, or by both together, unaccompanied.

29 | God, who made the stars of heaven

Ruth Duck, USA

THIAN BENG 85 85 85 75
I-to Loh, Taiwan

♩ = 100

God, who made the stars of hea-ven, God who spread the earth,
Gott, du machst die Him-mels-ster-ne, machst die Er - de weit.
Toi, qui as cré - é la ter-re le mon - de et les cieux.

breath of ev-ery liv-ing be-ing, fount of life_ and birth,
A - tem al - ler Le - be - we - sen, Quel-le al - ler Zeit,
Sour - ce de tou - te lu - miè - re, qui bril-le en tout lieu.

you have formed a ser-vant peo-ple, lead us by your hand.
du hast dir_ ein Volk ge - ru - fen, führst mit gu - ter_ Hand.
Tu nous fais_ peu - ple de frè - res, gui - dés par ta_ main.

Light of na-tions, shine in us; brigh-ten ev - ery_ land.
Licht der Völ-ker, schein in uns ü - ber je - dem Land.
Ser - vi-teurs d'un mê-me Pè-re, peu - ple de té - moins.

English

1 God, who made the stars of heaven,
God who spread the earth,
breath of every living being,
fount of life and birth,
you have formed a servant people,
led us by your hand.
Light of nations, shine in us;
brighten every land.

2 Living Christ, the light of nations,
radiant as the sun,
build us up, a growing body;
knit your church as one.
May our loving be a witness
all the world may see.
Send your Spirit, bond of peace,
source of unity.

3 Spirit God, equip your people,
all with gifts to share:
messengers to speak the gospel,
ministers of care.
So may valleys rise to greatness,
mountains be a plain.
Come, surprise us; change our lives;
heal each heart in pain.

4 So may nations praise your greatness,
do your will on earth,
free the captives from their prisons,
treat the poor with worth.
So may desert, coast and village
sing new songs to you.
Light of nations, fill the world,
making all things new.

(German and French verses overleaf)

German

1 Gott, du machst die Himmelssterne,
machst die Erde weit.
Atem aller Lebewesen,
Quelle aller Zeit,
du hast dir ein Volk gerufen,
führst mit guter Hand.
Licht der Völker, schein in uns
über jedem Land.

2 Christus, Leben, Licht der Völker,
bist wie Sonnenschein.
Bau uns auf, ein Volk im Wachsen,
lass uns einig sein.
Uns're Liebe sei ein Zeugnis,
das die Welt kann sehn.
Schick den Geist als Friedensband,
aus dem Einheit kommt.

3 Gottesgeist, hilf deinen Leuten,
teil die Gaben aus;
wir sind Boten deiner Nachricht,
dienen deinem Haus.
Mögen Täler sich erhöhen,
Berge eben sein.
Komm, erfüll uns, ändre Leben,
heile Seelenleid.

4 Mögen Völker dich erhöhen,
hör'n auf dein Gebot,
aus den Kerkern Gefang'ne holen,
lindern Armer Not.
Mögen Wüste, Küste, Städte
singen ein neues Lied.
Licht der Völker, füll die Erde,
und mach alles neu.

tr. Wolfgang Leyk

French

1 Toi, qui as créé la terre
le monde et les cieux.
Source de toute lumière,
qui brille en tout lieu.
Tu nous fais peuple de frères,
guidés par ta main.
Serviteurs d'un même Père,
peuple de témoins.

2 Jésus-Christ tu es la vie
et tu es la joie.
Tous les croyants tu les lies
dans la même foi.
Ton amour qui nous fait vivre,
le monde le voit.
Ton Esprit qui nous délivre,
nous unit en Toi.

3 Esprit-Saint rends-nous dociles
à tes volontés.
Pour prêcher ton Evangile
dans la verité.
Viens aplanir tous les sentiers,
hausser les vallées.
Viens nous aimer et consoler
les cœurs oppressés.

4 Tous les peuples tu les sauves
dans le monde entier.
Tu rends libres tous les pauvres
et les opprimés.
C'est ta croix qui est le gage
d'un amour si grand.
Ta joie qui nous rend sages
pour toujours vivants.

tr. Jacques Fischer

30

Haleluya Puji Tuhan

Trad. Soahuku, Indonesia
adapt. Christian I. Tamaela

♩ = 108

(Alleluia, praise the Lord.)

(Halleluja, lobet den Herrn.)

(Alléluia, louez le Seigneur.)

(¡Aleluya, alabado sea Dios!)

31

Healing is flowing, deep in the waters

Norman C. Habel, Australia

BUNESSAN 55 54 D
Trad., Scotland

English

1 Healing is flowing, deep in the waters,
   healing from Eden, flowing from old;
   all through creation, God sends forth waters,
   oceans of healing, for all the world.

2 Healing is rising, fresh with the morning,
   healing is rising, bursting with grace;
   Christ, as you surge from deep in creation,
   heal Earth's deep wounds and rise in this place.

3 Healing is breathing, life from the Spirit,
   healing is breathing, making flesh whole;
   breath of the Spirit, blow through our churches,
   come, heal our people, body and soul.

4 Healing is offered, leaves from the life tree,
   healing is offered nations at war;
   come, wounded Healer, torn by the violence,
   break down the walls, bring peace to our shore.

5 Healing is flowing, free with Christ's body,
   healing is flowing, free with Christ's blood;
   may this deep power pulse through our bodies,
   heal the world's wounds, still bleeding and red.

German

1 Heilung strömt zu uns, durch alle Wasser,
   Heilung vom Anfang, Heilung für uns.
   Kräfte der Heilung wirken für immer,
   in seiner ganzen Schöpfung für uns.

2 Heilung beginnt neu, an jedem Morgen,
   wenn frische Kräfte sammeln sich neu.
   Tief in der Schöpfung, da wirkst du, Christus,
   verbinde Wunden, die Welt mach heil.

3 Heilung heisst atmen im Geist des Lebens,
   Körper und Seele finden zur Ruh,
   Sende den Geist, Gott, in deine Kirche,
   dass sie nicht fürchte Nachteil und Macht.

4 Heilung vollzieht sich nicht ohne Opfer,
   Umkehr und Wandel verlangen viel.
   Länder im Kriege, lasst euch bekehren,
   seht zu dem einen Friedensfürst hin!

5 Heilung fliesst durch uns, die wir verbunden,
   in Christi Leib die Kirche wir sind.
   Seine Kraft wirke durch unser Leben,
   dass wir ein Mittel der Heilung sind.
   tr. Dietrich Werner

French

1 Guéris ce monde, Dieu des fontaines,
   Dieu de la source, des océans;
   nettoie nos fautes, lave nos peines;
   guéris ce monde, sois bienfaisant.

2 Guéris ce monde, Dieu qui relève,
   et que ta force nous soit donnée;
   ta grâce abonde, le Christ se lève;
   guéris ce monde par ta bonté.

3 Guéris ce monde, Dieu de la vie,
   envoie ton souffle sur toute chair;
   qu'il se répande par nos Églises;
   guéris ce monde de ses misères.

4 Guéris ce monde, Dieu qui demande,
   au lieu des guerres, enfin la paix;
   viens mettre un terme à la violence;
   guéris ce monde à tout jamais.

5 Guéris ce monde, Dieu qui libère,
   par le corps du Christ, et par son sang;
   que sa présence nous régénère;
   guéris ce monde dès maintenant.
   tr. Marc Chambron

32
Ikke ved makt

Sverre Therkelsen

Knut Nystedt, Norway

Ik - ke ved makt—   ik - ke ved vold og ved   makt vil du   rå - de,
Ne - ver by might,   ne - ver by vio-lence or   might do you   rule   us,
Nie-mals mit Macht,   nie mit Ge-walt und mit   Macht du uns   füh - re!

nei, ved din nå - de,   ja, ved din kjær - li - ge   hånd   og   din   nå - de!
but by your mer - cy,   yes, by your mer - ci - ful   hand   and   com - pas - sion.
Gott, uns be - rüh - re!   Uns mit der lie-ben-den   Hand   uns   be - rüh - re!

Norwegian

1 Ikke ved makt — ikke ved vold og ved makt vil du råde,
  nei, ved din nåde, ja, ved din kjærlige hånd og din nåde!

2 Ikke ved sverd — ikke ved ild og ved sverd du oss bøye!
  Nei, ved ditt øye, ja, ved et faderlig blikk fra ditt øye.

3 Ikke ved frykt — ikke ved redsel og frykt vil du lede,
  nei, ved din glede, ja, ved det sinn som du fyller med glede!

4 Ikke ved dom — ikke forstøt oss til trelldom og trengsel!
  Nei, gi oss lengsel! Styr våre hjerter ved håp og ved lengsel!

English

1 Never by might, never by violence or might do you rule us,
  but by your mercy, yes, by your merciful hand and compassion.

2 Never with sword, never with fire or with sword do you force us,
  but with your vision, yes, with the gaze of your love do you draw us.

3 Never by fear, never by terror or fear do you drive us,
  but by your gladness, yes, by our souls filled with joy do you lead us.

4 Never by threat, never by menace or threat do you sway us.
  Urge us to seek you, filling our hearts with your hope and your longing.
        tr. Maggie Hamilton

German

1 Niemals mit Macht, nie mit Gewalt und mit Macht du uns führe!
  Gott, uns berühre! Uns mit der liebenden Hand uns berühre!

2 Niemals mit Schwert, niemals mit Flammen und Schwertern uns leite!
  Du uns begleite, uns mit dem Vaterblick zärtlich begleite!

3 Niemals mit Furcht, nie willst mit Gräuel und Furcht du uns biegen.
  Freude wir kriegen! Freiheit und Freude im Herzen wir kriegen.

4 Niemals mit Zwang, spar uns den Zwang und die ängstlichen Tränen!
  Nur lass uns sehnen! Lass nach Erlösung uns zutraulich sehnen!
        tr. Sverre Therkelsen

33

Iloitse, maa! (Halleluja–laulu)

based on Psalm 100

Words and music by
Olli Kortekangas, Finland

I - loit - se, maa!__ Her - ral - le
All the earth, praise!_ Serve God with
Jauch - ze, o Er - de! Die - net dem
Toi, ter - re en - tière, ac - cla - me

rie - mu - huu - - to ko - hot - ta - kaa!
heart and soul__ and sing out your joy!
Herrn mit Freu - - den, froh - lo - cket ihm!
le Sei - gneur,__ et chan - te ta joie!

INSTRUMENT (ad lib.)

Hal - le - lu - ja, hal - le - lu - ja, hal - le - lu - ja! Aa
Al - le - lu - ia, al - le - lu - ia, al - le - lu - ia! A_____
Hal - le - lu - ja, hal - le - lu - ja, hal - le - lu - ja! A_____
Al - lé - lu - ia, al - lé - lu - ia, al - lé - lu - ia! A_____

Hal - le - lu - ja,   hal - le - lu - ja,   hal - le - lu - ja! Aa - men.
Al - le - lu - ia,   al - le - lu - ia,   al - le - lu - ia! A - men.
Hal - le - lu - ja,   hal - le - lu - ja,   hal - le - lu - ja! A - men.
Al - lé - lu - ia,   al - lé - lu - ia,   al - lé - lu - ia! A - men.

Finnish

1 Iloitse, maa!
 Herralle riemuhuuto kohottakaa!
 Halleluja, halleluja, halleluja!
 Halleluja, halleluja, halleluja! Aamen.

2 Ylistä, maa!
 Porteilleen kiitoslauluin vaeltakaa!

3 Taivas ja maa
 alati Herran voimaa julistakaa!

English

1 All the earth, praise!
 Serve God with heart and soul
  and sing out your joy!
 Alleluia, alleluia, alleluia!
 Alleluia, alleluia, alleluia! Amen.

2 All the earth's people,
 enter the gates of God with thanks
  and with praise!

3 Heaven and earth,
 sing of the power of God, Creator of all!
 tr. Maggie Hamilton

German

1 Jauchze, o Erde!
 Dienet dem Herrn mit Freuden,
  frohlocket ihm!
 Halleluja, halleluja, halleluja!
 Halleluja, halleluja, halleluja! Amen.

2 Preise, o Erde!
 Kommt durch die Tore jauchzend,
  und danket ihm!

3 Himmel und Erde!
 Preiset den Herrn, den Schöpfer,
  lobt seine Macht!
 tr. Dietrich Werner

French

1 Toi, terre entière,
 acclame le Seigneur, et chante ta joie!
 Alléluia, alléluia, alléluia!
 Alléluia, alléluia, alléluia! Amen.

2 Vous, tous les peuples,
 venez dans sa maison, pour bénir son nom!

3 Vous, ciel et terre,
 chantez sa royauté, sa fidélité!
 tr. Marc Chambron

34 | I will live for you alone

Words and music by
Trisha Watts, Australia

I___ will live for you a-lone, for you a - lone I'll live.
Le - ben will ich dir al-lein, dein ist mein gan - zes Sein.
Pa - ra ti yo vi - vi - ré, tan só - lo pa - ra ti.

Heal me, heal me, heal me and let me live.
Heil mich, heil mich, heil mich und lass mich sein.
Sa - na, sa - na, sa-na mi vi - da ya.

German tr. Dorothea Wulfhorst; Spanish tr. Martin Junge

(Je vivrai pour toi seul. Guéris-moi et fais-moi vivre.)

35 Jeder Teil dieser Erde

Chief Seattle, native American

Stefan Vesper, Germany

Canon

1. Je - der Teil die - ser Er - de
   Ev - 'ry part of this earth
   Cha - que lieu sur cet - te ter - re
   Ca - da lu - gar de es - te mun - do

2. ist mei - nem Volk hei - lig.
   is to my peo - ple ho - ly.
   est pour mon peu - ple bien sa - cré.
   es lu - gar san - to pa - ra mi pueblo.

3. Je - der Teil die - ser Er - de
   Ev - 'ry part of this earth
   Cha - que lieu sur cet - te ter - re
   Ca - da lu - gar de es - te mun - do

4. ist mei - nem Volk hei - lig.
   is to my peo - ple ho - ly.
   est pour mon peu - ple bien sa - cré.
   es lu - gar san - to pa - ra mi pueblo.

36

Jesu neem un nu gu shin ga

Seong-Won Park

Sung-Mo Moon, Korea

Korean

1 Jesu neem un nu gu shin ga
  ug ab uee khol ja ki uee cha yoo uee kot
  ka nan han beck sung uee chin ku shi ra.

2 Jesu neem un nu gu shin ga
  chul mang uee ku nul so geh
    hee mang uee bit
  kee ree run beck sung uee mok cha shi ra.

3 Jesu neem un nu gu shin ga
  chun chaeng uee yok sa so geh pyung wha uee wang
  sum at kin beck sung uee saeng myung iee ra.

English

1 Jesus asks, 'Who do you say that I am?'
  Blossom of freedom in repression's
      dark vale,
  lover of justice, and friend of the poor.

2 Jesus asks, 'Who do you say that I am?'
  Beam of hope shining in the night of despair,
  guiding and tending all those who are lost.

3 Jesus asks, 'Who do you say that I am?'
  Maker of peace in the destruction of war;
  to all who suffer the Giver of Life.
                    tr. Maggie Hamilton

German

1 Du fragst uns Jesus: Wer bin ich für euch?
  Blüte der Freiheit, mitten in Not und Tod,
  Freund aller Armen und Heiland der Welt.

2 Du fragst uns Jesus: Wer bin ich für euch?
  Lichtblick der Hoffnung, trotz Trübsal
      und Furcht,
  Halt der Verzagten und Hirt der Verlor'n.

3 Du fragst uns Jesus: Wer bin ich für euch?
  Du stiftest Frieden überwindest Gewalt.
  Du stiftest Leben für alle im Leid.
                    tr. Dietrich Werner

French

1 Qui dites-vous que je suis, moi Jésus?
  Fleur de liberté, quand vous êtes opprimés,
  je suis l'ami des pauvres et leur soutien.

2 Qui dites-vous que je suis, moi Jésus?
  Lumière d'espoir, éclairant vos ténèbres,
  je suis le bon berger, je vous connais.

3 Qui dites-vous que je suis, moi Jésus?
  Prince de la paix, malgré toutes vos guerres,
  et pour tous les meurtris, je suis la vie.
                    tr. Marc Chambron

37

Jesus, Lamb of God (Agnus Dei)

Music and additional words by
Marty Haugen, USA

English

1 Jesus, Lamb of God,
   you take away the sins of the world:
   have mercy on us, O Lord.

2 Jesus, Word of God, …
3 Jesus, Bread of Life, …
4 Jesus, Cup of Life, …
5 Jesus, Light of Peace, …
6 Jesus, Hope of all, …
7 Jesus, Word made Flesh, …
8 Jesus, Morning Star, …
9 Jesus, Shepherd King, …
10 Jesus, First and Last, …

11 Jesus, Fire of Love, …
12 Jesus, Risen Lord, …
13 Jesus, Prince of Peace, …
14 Jesus, Breath of Life, …
15 Jesus, Light of Eyes, …
16 Jesus, Rising Son, …
17 Jesus, Bread from Heav'n, …
18 Jesus, Child of Peace, …
19 Jesus, Hope of All, …

German

1 Jesus, Gottes Lamm,
   du nimmst hinweg die Sünde der Welt:
   erbarme dich unser Herr.

2 Jesus, Gottes Wort, …
3 Jesus, Lebensbrot, …
4 Jesus, Lebenstrank, …
5 Jesus, Friedenslicht, …
6 Jesus, Hoffnungsschein, …
7 Fleischgeword'nes Wort, …
8 Jesus, Morgenstern, …
9 Jesus, guter Hirt, …
10 Jesus, A und O, …

11 Jesus, liebevoll, …
12 Auferstand'ner Herr, …
13 Jesus, Friedefürst, …
14 Jesus, Lebenshauch, …
15 Jesus, unser Licht, …
16 Jesus, auferweckt, …
17 Jesus, Himmelsbrot, …
18 Jesus, Friedenskraft, …
19 Hoffnung, stark wie Tod, …

tr. Angelika Joachim

(1. Jésus, Agneau de Dieu, *qui enlèves les péchés du monde: prends pitié de nous.* 2. Jésus, Parole de Dieu, … 3. Jésus, Pain de vie, … 4. Jésus, Coupe de la vie, … 5. Jésus, Lumière de la Paix, … 6. Jésus, Espoir de tous, … 7. Jésus, Parole faite chair, … 8. Jésus, Etoile du matin, … 9. Jésus, Roi des bergers, … 10. Jésus, le Premier et le Dernier, … 11. Jésus, Feu d'amour, … 12. Jésus, Seigneur ressuscité, … 13. Jésus, Prince de la Paix, … 14. Jésus, Souffle de vie, … 15. Jésus, Lumière de nos yeux, … 16. Jésus, Fils ressuscité, … 17. Jésus, Pain du ciel, … 18. Jésus, Enfant de Paix, … 19. Jésus, Espoir de tous, …)

38

Jesus, Lamb of God, bearer of our sin

Words and music by
Bernadette Farrell, England

English

1 Jesus, Lamb of God, bearer of our sin; Jesus, Saviour:
   Hear our prayer, hear our prayer; through this bread and wine we share
   may we be your sign of peace everywhere.

2 Jesus, Lamb of God, bearer of our pain; Jesus, healer:
3 Jesus, Lamb of God, broken as our bread, here among us:
4 Jesus, Lamb of God, poured out as our wine, shared in gladness:
5 Jesus, Word of God, dwelling with the poor; Jesus, prophet:
6 Jesus, Word of God, dwelling in our midst, Jesus with us:
7 Jesus, Word of God, speaking in our hearts God's compassion:
8 Jesus, Word made flesh, touching each one's need; Jesus, lover:
9 Kneeling by your friends, washing each one's feet; Jesus, servant:
10 Hope beyond despair, dawn of fragile light; Jesus, risen:
11 Tomb of secret hope, open to the dawn; Jesus, living:

German

1 Jesus, Gottes Lamm, du trägst uns're Schuld, Jesus Retter:
   Nähre uns, nähre uns, Brot und Wein des neuen Bunds
   seien Kraft und Stärkung für das Zeugnis uns.

2 Jesus, Gottes Lamm, du trägst unser Leid, Jesus Heiland:
3 Jesus, Gottes Lamm, du bist unser Brot, wirst gebrochen:
4 Jesus, Gottes Lamm, du bist unser Wein, wirst vergossen:
5 Jesus, Gottes Wort, bist den Armen nah, weist die Wege:
6 Jesus, Gottes Wort, bist uns allen nah, bist Gott-mit-uns:
7 Jesus, Gottes Wort, sprichst in unser Herz Gottes Liebe:
8 Fleischgeword'nes Wort, du kennst uns're Not, bist voll Liebe:
9 Kniest demütig hin, wäscht die Füsse uns, aller Diener:
10 Hoffnung stark wie Tod, erstes Morgenlicht, Auferstand'ner:
11 Grab im Morgenlicht, der, der tot war, lebt, ist erstanden:
                    tr. Angelika Joachim

French

1 Christ, Agneau de Dieu, portant nos péchés, tu nous sauves:
   Par ce pain, par ce vin, fais de nous, Seigneur Jésus,
   des artisans de ta paix, à jamais.

2 Christ, Agneau de Dieu, toi qui viens guérir nos souffrances:
3 Christ, Agneau de Dieu, toi le pain rompu pour les hommes:
4 Christ, Agneau de Dieu, toi le vin versé, joie du monde:
5 Christ, Verbe de Dieu, toi l'ami des pauvres sur terre:
6 Christ, Verbe de Dieu, au milieu de nous, le prophète:
7 Christ, Verbe de Dieu, qui parle a nos cœurs de ton Père:
8 Parole incarnée, toi qui es amour et tendresse:
9 Toi le serviteur, qui viens à genoux, laver nos pieds:
10 Jésus, notre espoir, Christ ressuscité, vraie lumière:
11 Jésus, notre paix, Christ toujours vivant, notre Sauveur:
                    tr. Marc Chambron

39
Jézus a jó pásztor

Dóka Zoltán   Trajtler Gábor, Hungary

Jé-zus a jó pász-tor, ve-le me-gyünk. Ö-rök ir-gal-má-ról
Je-sus, Good Shep-herd, guide us through the day. Lead us with lov-ing grace,
Je-sus, der gu-te Hirt, mit dem wir gehen, sei-ne Barm-her-zig-keit,

é-ne-ke-lünk. Nyá-ja-dat ol-tal-mazd,
show us the way. Shel-ter your flock, O Lord,
sie lässt uns singen. Nimm dei-ne Herd' in acht,

nagy a ve-szély! Csen-des nyu-gal-mat adj, ha jön az éj!
your peo-ple hear. Grant us your peace-ful rest when night is near.
wir sind be-droht, gib uns die stil-le Ruh, wenn Nacht sich naht.

Hungarian

1 Jézus a jó pásztor, vele megyünk.
  Örök irgalmáról énekelünk.
  Nyájadat oltalmazd, nagy a veszély!
  Csendes nyugalmat adj, ha jön az éj!

2 Jézus a szőlőtő, ereje nagy.
  Nem él hiába, ki benne marad.
  Gyümölcsöt érleljen szereteted,
  Tenélküled néped mit se tehet!

3 Jézus világosság, messze ragyog.
  Fényéből élnek mind a csillagok.
  Bűnünket oszlasd el, nagy a sötét!
  Vezesd te jó útra mind, aki vét!

4 Jézus a békesség, fegyvere egy:
  A megbocsátó és hű szeretet!
  Békére vágyódik mind e világ,
  Félelmes ínségből hozzád kiált!

5 Jézus a kezdet és Jézus a vég!
  Hadd zengje ég és föld dicséretét!
  Vezess az ösvényen, maradj velünk,
  Míg örök fényedbe megérkezünk!

English

1 Jesus, Good Shepherd, guide us through the day.
  Lead us with loving grace, show us the way.
  Shelter your flock, O Lord, your people hear.
  Grant us your peaceful rest when night is near.

2 Jesus, the True Vine, we're rooted in you;
  earth us in truth, Lord, then nurture us too.
  Strengthen our faith in distress and in strife;
  we are your branches, in you we have life.

3 Jesus, the Light of all, shine through our world.
  Heavenly stars praise you, radiant Lord.
  Shatter injustice and free us from wrong.
  Light in our darkness, your love is our song.

4 Jesus, our Peace, you're no hawk, but a dove
  granting forgiveness, and healing with love.
  Challenge our apathy, sharpen our will,
  give us the courage to overcome ill.

5 Shepherd and True Vine, our Peace and our Light,
  move through our world, spreading mercy and right.
  Giver of hope and love, bless us always;
  Alpha and Omega, we sing your praise.
            tr. Maggie Hamilton

German

1 Jesus, der gute Hirt, mit dem wir gehen,
  seine Barmherzigkeit, sie lässt uns singen.
  Nimm deine Herd' in acht, wir sind bedroht,
  gib uns die stille Ruh, wenn Nacht sich naht.

2 Jesus, dem Weinstock gleich, hat grosse Kraft,
  dass nicht umsonst gelebt, wer an ihm bleibt.
  Bringen soll viele Frucht die Kraft der Liebe.
  Ohne dich kann dein Volk gar nichts ausrichten.

3 Jesus, das Licht der Welt, strahlt weit hinaus.
  Das Heer der Sterne lebt von seinem Licht.
  Lösch uns're schwere Schuld, das grosse Dunkel.
  Bring wieder auf den Weg, die ihn verfehlten.

4 Jesus, dein Friede hat nur eine Waffe,
  die Liebe, die vergibt und die uns treu bleibt.
  Es sehnt nach Frieden sich uns're Welt,
  sie schreit zu dir den Schrei aus Angst und Not.

5 Weil Jesus Anfang ist, Jesus das Ende,
  singt Erd und Himmel ihm ein ew'ges Lob.
  Führ uns auf deinen Weg und bleibe bei uns,
  bis wir in deinem Licht zu Hause sind.
            tr. Gyula Cseri and Dieter Trautwein

Jikelele

Trad. Zulu, South Africa

(I know Jesus, he travels all around the world.)
(Ich kenne Jesus, er reist um die ganze Welt.)
(Je connais Jésus, il voyage à travers le monde entier.)
(Conozco a Jesús. El viaja por todo el mundo.)

41 Jyothi dho Prabhu

Words and music by
Charles Vas, India

♩ = 120

Jyo - thi dho, jyo - thi dho, jyo - thi dho__ Pra - bhu.__
Give_ us light, give__ us light, give_ us light,_ O Lord.__
Gib_ uns Licht, gib__ uns Licht, gib_ uns Licht,_ o Herr.__

Jyo - thi dho Pra - bhu,_____ jyo - thi dho,
Give__ us light, O__ Lord,_____ give____ us light,
Gib__ uns Licht, o__ Herr,_____ gib_____ uns Licht,

jyo - thi dho, jyo - thi dho_____ Pra - bhu._____
give____ us light, give_ us light,__ O Lord._____
gib_____ uns Licht, gib_ uns Licht,__ o Herr._____

Hindhi

1 Jyothi dho, jyothi dho, jyothi dho Prabhu.
Jyothi dho, jyothi dho, jyothi dho Prabhu.
Jyothi dho Prabhu,
jyothi dho, jyothi dho, jyothi dho Prabhu.

2 Jiivan dho, …   4 Mukthi dho, …

3 Shanthi dho, …   5 Aasish dho, …

English

1 Give us light, give us light, give us light, O Lord.
Give us light, give us light, give us light, O Lord.
Give us light, O Lord,
give us light, give us light, give us light, O Lord.

2 Give us life, …   4 Save us now, …

3 Grant us peace, …   5 Give us grace, …

German

1 Gib uns Licht, gib uns Licht, gib uns Licht, o Herr.
Gib uns Licht, gib uns Licht, gib uns Licht, o Herr.
Gib uns Licht, o Herr,
gib uns Licht, gib uns Licht, gib uns Licht, o Herr.

2 Gib uns Sinn, …   4 Hilf uns nun, …

3 Gib uns Halt, …   5 Gib uns Mut, …

tr. Päivi Jussila

42

Khudaya, rahem kar

R. F. Liberius, Pakistan

♩ = 102

1,3. Khu - da - ya, ra - hem kar.__ Khu - da - ya ra -

- hem, khu - da - ya,__ ra - hem kar. Khu - da - ya__ ra -

Fine

- hem. Khu - da - ya ra - hem kar,__ khu - da - ya ra - hem.

2. Ma - si - ha,__ ra - hem kar, ma - si - ha,__ ra -

- hem. Ma - si - ha ra - hem kar, ma - si - ha,__ ra -

D.C.

- hem. Ma - si - ha, ra - hem kar,__ ma - si - ha, ra - hem.

(1,3. Lord, have mercy. 2. Christ, have mercy.)

(1,3. Herr, erbarme dich. 2. Christus, erbarme dich.)

(1,3. Seigneur, aie pitié. 2. Christ, aie pitié.)

(1,3. Señor, ten piedad. 2. Cristo, ten piedad.)

Sung unaccompanied

Kyrie eleison

Dinah Reindorf, Ghana

Ky - ri - e e - le - i - son, Ky - ri - e e - le - i - son,

Ky - ri - e e - le - i - son, Ky - ri - e e - le - i - son.

(Lord, have mercy.)

(Herr, erbarme dich.)

(Seigneur, aic pitié de nous.)

(Señor, ten piedad de nosotros.)

44

Kiedy ranne wstają zorze

Franciszek Karpinski

Unknown, Poland

Kie - dy ran - ne wsta - ją zo - rze, To - bie zie - mia, To - bie mo - rze.
In the dis - tance day is break - ing, earth and sea a glad sound mak - ing.
Mor-gen-rö - te scheint von Fer - ne, Erd und Meer dich prei - sen ger - ne,

To-bie śpie - wa ży-wioł wszel - ki: Bądź po-chwa-lon, Bo - że wiel - ki!
All cre - a - tion joined in sing - ing, God, to you, praise and thanks bring - ing.
al - le Le - be - we-sen sin - gen: Dir, Gott, soll das Lob - lied klin - gen!

Polish

1 Kiedy ranne wstają zorze,
Tobie ziemia, Tobie morze.
Tobie śpiewa żywioł wszelki:
Bądź pochwalon, Boże wielki!

2 Ledwie oczy przetrzeć zdołam,
wnet do mego Pana wołam,
do mego Boga na niebie
i szukam Go koło siebie.

3 Wielu snem śmierci upadli,
co się wczoraj spać pokładli,
my się jeszcze obudzili,
byśmy Cię, Boże, chwalili.

English

1 In the distance day is breaking,
 earth and sea a glad sound making.
 All creation joined in singing,
 God, to you, praise and thanks bringing.

2 Lord, before you I am standing,
 your hand grasping, love adoring,
 your own dwelling I will enter,
 you, my God, my own life's centre.

3 Friends who walk with us no longer,
 held by death, yet love is stronger.
 Day dawns bright, new hope extending,
 thanks to God in praise unending.
 tr. Jeffrey T. Myers

German

1 Morgenröte scheint von Ferne,
 Erd und Meer dich preisen gerne,
 alle Lebewesen singen:
 Dir, Gott, soll das Loblied klingen!

2 Vor dich will ich heute treten,
 dich, den Herren, anzubeten,
 meinen Gott im Himmel droben
 such ich heut und will ihn loben.

3 Viele sind von uns gegangen,
 noch hält sie der Tod gefangen.
 Weil wir wach den Tag erblicken,
 woll'n wir frühes Lob dir schicken.
 tr. Tadeusz Sikora

45

Komm, Herr, segne uns

Words and music by
Dieter Trautwein, Germany

Komm, Herr, seg - ne uns, dass wir uns nicht tren - nen,
Bless and keep us, Lord, in your love u - ni - ted,
Viens et nous bé - nis, Dieu de la ren - con - tre,

son - dern ü - ber - all uns zu dir be - ken - nen.
from your fa - mi - ly ne - ver se - par - a - ted.
c'est toi qui u - nis, ton a - mour le mon - tre,

Nie sind wir al - lein,_____ stets sind wir die Dei - nen,
You make all things new_____ as we fol - low af - ter;
gar - de tes en - fants_____ au creux des tem - pê - tes,

La - chen o - der Wei - nen wird ge - seg - net sein.
whe - ther tears or laugh - ter, we be - long to you.
comme au temps des fê - tes sois tou - jours pré - sent.

English translation © 1985 Stainer & Bell Ltd

German

1 Komm, Herr, segne uns,
    dass wir uns nicht trennen,
sondern überall uns zu dir bekennen.
Nie sind wir allein, stets sind wir die Deinen,
Lachen oder Weinen wird gesegnet sein.

2 Keiner kann allein Segen sich bewahren.
Weil du reichlich gibst,
    müssen wir nicht sparen.
Segen kann gedeihn, wo wir alles teilen,
schlimmen Schaden heilen,
    lieben und verzeihn.

3 Frieden gabst du schon,
    Frieden muss noch werden,
wie du ihn versprichst uns zum Wohl auf Erden.
Hilf, dass wir ihn tun, wo wir ihn erspähen;
die mit Tränen säen, werden in ihm ruhn.

4 Komm, Herr, segne uns,
    dass wir uns nicht trennen,
sondern überall uns zu dir bekennen.
Nie sind wir allein, stets sind wir die Deinen,
Lachen oder Weinen wird gesegnet sein.

English

1 Bless and keep us, Lord,
    in your love united,
from your family never separated.
You make all things new as we follow after;
whether tears or laughter, we belong to you.

2 Blessing shrivels up when
    your children hoard it;
help us, Lord, to share, for we can afford it:
blessing only grows in the act of sharing,
in a life of caring, love that heals and glows.

3 Fill your world with peace,
    such as you intended.
Teach us prize the earth, love, replenish, tend it.
Lord, uplift, fulfil all who sow in sadness:
let them reap with gladness, by your kingdom thrilled.

4 Bless and keep us, Lord,
    in your love united,
from your family never separated.
You make all things new as we follow after;
whether tears or laughter, we belong to you.
tr. Fred Kaan

French

1 Viens et nous bénis, Dieu de la rencontre,
c'est toi qui unis, ton amour le montre,
garde tes enfants au creux des tempêtes,
comme au temps des fêtes sois
    toujours présent.

2 Tes dons généreux, ta surabondance
pour les malheureux ouvrent une danse.
Feu qui nous saisit porte témoignage!
Esprit de partage, viens, ô Jésus-Christ.

3 Porteur de la paix, la paix que tu donnes,
semeurs désormais pour le bien des hommes.
Nous voulons, Seigneur, dans la vigilance
que ton règne avance, toi, le vrai bonheur.

4 Viens et nous bénis, Dieu de la rencontre,
c'est toi qui unis, ton amour le montre,
garde tes enfants au creux des tempêtes,
comme au temps des fêtes sois toujours présent.
tr. M. L. Munger and L. Levis

La ténèbre

based on Psalm 139: 12

Jacques Berthier
for the Taizé Community, France

La té - nè - bre n'est point té - nè - bre de - vant toi: la
Our__ dark - ness is ne - ver dark - ness in your sight: the
Die__ Fin - ster - nis ist nicht fin - ster für__ dich. Die
La ti - nie - bla ya no es ti - nie - bla an - te ti, la

nuit com - me le jour est lu - miè - - re.
deep - est night is clear as the day - - light.
Nacht__ ist__ Licht wie der Tag._____
no - che co - mo el dí - a i - lu - mi - - na.

Lamb of God

Barrie Cabena, Canada

Lamb__ of__ God,__ you take a - way_ the__
A - gneau de__ Dieu,__ qui en - lè - ves_ les__
Got - tes__ Lamm,__ du nimmst hin - weg_ die__

sins_____ of the world:___ have mer - cy on us.
pé - chés du__ monde:___ prends pi - tié de nous.
Sün - den der__ Welt:_____ er - barme dich un - ser.

world:_____ grant_____ us__ peace.
monde:_____ ac - cor - de - nous_ la__ paix.
Welt:_____ Frie - - den gib_____ uns.

French tr. Marc Chambron; German tr. Dietrich Werner

(Cordero de Dios, que quitas el pecado del mundo: ten piedad de nosotros. Cordero de Dios, que quitas el pecado del mundo: danos tu paz.)

For performance by congregation and/or choir, with organ, or by a cantor with the congregation responding 'have mercy on us' and 'grant us peace'.

48 | Laudate omnes gentes

Psalm 117: 1

Jacques Berthier
for the Taizé Community, France

Lau - da - te om-nes gen - tes, lau - da - te Do-mi - num. Lau -

-da - te om-nes gen - tes, lau - da - te Do-mi - num.

UPPER VOICE VERSION

Lau - da - te om-nes gen - tes, lau - da - te Do - mi -

- num. Lau - da - te om-nes gen - tes, lau - da - te Do-mi - num!

(All peoples, praise the Lord!)

(Lobet alle Völker, lobet den Herrn!)

(Louez le Seigneur, tous les peuples!)

(¡Pueblos todos alabad al Señor!)

Le Seigneur fit pour moi des merveilles

Luke 1: 49 (French)

Joseph Gélineau, France

Le Sei - gneur fit pour moi des mer - veil - les: Saint est son nom.
Might-y God, you have called me to serve you: Ho - ly your name!
Gu - ter Gott, du rufst mich, dir zu die - nen. Eh - re sei dir!

English tr. Fred Kaan; German tr. Dietrich Werner

(El Señor ha hecho en mí grandes cosas ¡Santo es su nombre!)

50 | Let my prayer rise before you

Psalm 141: 2

David Schack, USA

Let my prayer rise be-fore___ you as in - cense;
Mein Ge - bet stei - ge zu dir, Gott, zum Him - mel.
Ma pri - ère com - me l'en - cens mon - te vers toi,
Su - ba a ti mi o - ra - ción___ co - mo in - cien - so,

the lift - ing up of my hands as the eve-ning sac - ri - fice.
Die Hän - de heb ich zu dir, sag dir Dank für die - sen Tag.
vers toi mes mains se lè - vent en sa - cri - fi - ce le soir.
al - za - das ma - nos sean mi sa - cri - fi - cio de la tarde.

German tr. Dietrich Werner; French tr. Marc Chambron; Spanish tr. Martin Junge

51 | Let there be light

Frances Wheeler Davis

CONCORD   47 76
Robert J. B. Fleming, Canada

Let there be light,_____ let there be un - der - stand - ing,
Licht füll die Welt,_____ den Völ-kern wach - se Hoff - nung,

let all the na - tions gath - er, let them be face to face.
Kul - tu-ren und Na - tion - en rei - chen ein-ander die Hand.

English

1 Let there be light, let there be understanding,
  let all the nations gather, let them be face to face.

2 Open our lips, open our minds to ponder,
  open the door of concord opening into grace.

3 Perish the sword, perish the angry judgement,
  perish the bombs and hunger, perish the fight for gain.

4 Hallow our love, hallow the deaths of martyrs,
  hallow their holy freedom, hallowed be your name.

5 Your kingdom come, your spirit turn to language,
  your people speak together, your spirit never fade.

6 Let there be light, open our hearts to wonder,
  perish the way of terror, hallow the world God made.

German

1 Licht füll die Welt, den Völkern wachse Hoffnung,
  Kulturen und Nationen reichen einander die Hand.

2 Schliesst auf die Tür, die Arm und Reich noch trennen,
  öffnet dem Leben Chancen, Schuldenerlass bringt ein.

3 Hass, den lasst sein! Gebt der Gewalt den Abschied.
  Bomben und Hunger ächtet, Kampf muss nicht länger sein.

4 Liebe gebt Raum, ihre Zeugen achtet!
  Ihre Freiheit schützet! Ihren Kreis macht weit!

5 Gott, dein Reich komm! Dein Geist berühr die Menschen,
  dass Worte Flügel kriegen und Fronten überspring'.

6 Licht füll die Welt, den Herzen wachse Hoffnung,
  Terror und Mord verschwinde, lass endlich Frieden sein.
                    tr. Dietrich Werner

52 | Let us break bread together

10 10 with refrain
Trad., African American
arr. Gerre Hancock

Let us break bread to-ge-ther on our
Lasst uns Brot bre - chen und Gott dank - bar
De ro - dil - las par - ta-mos hoy el

knees.
sein.
pan.

Let us break bread to-ge-ther on our
Lasst uns Brot bre - chen und Gott dank - bar
De ro - dil - las par - ta-mos hoy el

knees.
sein.
pan.

When I fall on my knees with my
Wenn ich kni - e und he - be den
De ro - dil - las es-toy con el

face to the ri - sing sun, O Lord, have mer - cy on me.
Blick in des Lich - tes Schein, dann, Herr, er - bar - me dich mein!
ros - tro al na - cien - te sol. Oh Dios, a - piá - da - te de mi!

English

1 Let us break bread together on our knees.
Let us break bread together on our knees.
When I fall on my knees with my face to the rising sun,
O Lord, have mercy on me.

2 Let us drink wine together on our knees. ...

3 Let us praise God together on our knees. ...

German

1 Lasst uns Brot brechen und Gott dankbar sein.
Lasst uns Brot brechen und Gott dankbar sein.
Wenn ich knie und hebe den Blick in des Lichtes Schein,
dann, Herr, erbarme dich mein!

2 Nehmt den Kelch, trinkt und lasst uns dankbar sein. ...

3 Lasst uns Gott loben und ihm dankbar sein. ...
tr. Dieter Trautwein

Spanish

1 De rodillas partamos hoy el pan.
De rodillas partamos hoy el pan.
De rodillas estoy con el rostro al naciente sol.
Oh Dios, apiádate de mi!

2 Compartamos la copa en gratitud. ...

3 De rodillas loemos al Señor. ...
tr. Federico Pagura

53
Lobe den Herren

LOBE DEN HERREN 14 14 4 7 8
Words by, and melody adapt. by
Joachim Neander, Germany

Lo - be den Her - ren, den mäch - ti - gen Kö - nig der Eh - ren; lob ihn, o
Praise to the Lord, the Al - migh - ty, the King of cre - a - tion! O my soul,
Peup - les, cri - ez de joie et bon - dis - sez d'al - lé - gres - se. Le Pè - re en -
Al - ma, ben - di - ce al Se - ñor, Dios po - ten - te de glo - ria; de sus mer -

See - le, ver - eint mit den himm - li - schen Chö - ren. Kom - met zu -
praise him, for he is your health and sal - va - tion! Let all who
- voie son Fils ma - ni - fes - ter sa ten - dres - se. Ou - vrons les
- ce - des es - té vi - va en ti la me - mo - ria. Oh des - per -

- hauf: Psal - ter und Har - fe, wacht auf. Las - set den Lob - ge - sang hö - ren.
hear now to his tem - ple draw near, join - ing in glad a - do - ra - tion.
yeux: il est l'i - ma - ge de Dieu! Pour que cha - cun le con - nais - se!
- tad, con voz de go - zo can - tad him - nos de ho - nor y vic - to - ria.

German

1 Lobe den Herren, den mächtigen König der Ehren;
lob ihn, o Seele, vereint mit den himmlischen Chören.
Kommet zuhauf:
Psalter und Harfe, wacht auf.
Lasset den Lobgesang hören.

2 Lobe den Herren, der alles so herrlich regieret,
der dich auf Adelers Fittichen sicher geführet,
der dich erhält,
wie es dir selber gefällt.
Hast du nicht dieses verspüret?

3 Lobe den Herren, der deinen Stand sichtbar gesegnet,
der aus dem Himmel mit Strömen der Liebe geregnet.
Denke daran,
was der Allmächtige kann,
der dir mit Liebe begegnet!

4 Lobe den Herren, was in mir ist, lobe den Namen.
Lob ihn mit allen, die seine Verheissung bekamen.
Er ist dein Licht;
Seele, vergiss es ja nicht.
Lob ihn in Ewigkeit. Amen.

English

1 Praise to the Lord, the Almighty, the King of creation!
O my soul, praise him, for he is your health and salvation!
Let all who hear
now to his temple draw near,
joining in glad adoration.

2 Praise to the Lord, who o'er all things is wondrously reigning,
and, as on wings of an eagle, uplifting, sustaining;
have you not seen
all that is needful has been
sent by his gracious ordaining?

3 Praise to the Lord, who will prosper your work and defend you;
surely his goodness and mercy shall daily attend you;
ponder anew
what the Almighty can do,
if with his love he befriend you.

4 Praise to the Lord! O let all that is in me adore him!
All that has life and breath, come now with praises before him!
Let the amen
sound from his people again:
gladly forever adore him.

tr. Catherine Winkworth (altd.)

(*French and Spanish verses overleaf*)

French

1 Peuples, criez de joie et bondissez d'allégresse.
Le Père envoie son Fils manifester sa tendresse.
Ouvrons les yeux:
il est l'image de Dieu!
Pour que chacun le connaisse!

2 Loué soit notre Dieu, Source et Parole fécondes;
ses mains ont tout créé pour que nos cœurs lui répondent;
par Jésus Christ
il donne l'être et la vie,
en nous sa vie surabonde.

3 Loué soit notre Dieu, dont la splendeur se révèle
quand nous buvons le vin pour une terre nouvelle;
par Jésus Christ
le monde passe aujourd'hui
vers une gloire éternelle.

4 Peuples, battez des mains et proclamez votre fête:
le Père accueille en lui ceux que son Verbe rachète;
dans l'Esprit Saint
par qui vous n'êtes plus qu'un,
que votre joie soit parfaite!
tr. Didier Rimaud

Spanish

1 Alma, bendice al Señor, Dios potente de gloria;
de sus mercedes esté viva en ti la memoria.
Oh despertad,
con voz de gozo cantad
himnos de honor y victoria.

2 Alma, bendice al Señor que a los astros gobierna
y te conduce paciente con mano paterna.
Te perdonó,
de todo mal te libró,
porque su gracia es eterna.

3 Alma, bendice al Señor, de tu vida la fuente,
que te creó y en salud te sostiene clemente;
tu sanador
en todo trance y dolor;
su diestra es omnipotente.

4 Alma, bendice al Señor por su amor infinito;
con todo el pueblo de Dios su alabanza repito;
Dios, mi salud,
de todo bien plenitud,
¡seas por siempre bendito!
tr. Federico Fliedner (altd.)

54

Louvai ao Senhor

Equipe do CELMU   Simei Pereira do Amaral, Brazil

Baião ♩ = 106

| Portuguese | English |

Portuguese

Louvai ao Senhor porque ele é bom!
Louvai ao Senhor porque ele é bom!

1 Pela fraternidade.

2 Pela paz e unidade.

3 Pelo amor e justiça.

4 Pela graça da vida.

English

We praise you, O God, because you are good!
We praise you, O God, because you are good!

1 You inspire faith and courage.

2 You bring nations together.

3 You inspire love and justice.

4 You inspire hope and vision.
                                    tr. Fred Kaan

German

Wir loben dich, Herr, denn du bist gut!
Wir loben dich, Herr, denn du bist gut!

1 Du bringst uns Gemeinschaft.

2 Du gibst Segen und Frieden.

3 Du schenkst Einheit und Liebe.

4 Du sorgst für Gerechtigkeit.
                                    tr. Ari Kuebelkamp

French

Louez le Seigneur, chantez sa bonté!
Louez le Seigneur, chantez sa bonté!

1 Pour la vie et pour l'amitié.

2 Pour la paix et pour l'unité.

3 Pour la justice et pour l'amour.

4 Pour sa grâce de chaque jour.
                                    tr. Marc Chambron

Baião

Instruments: accordion, zabumba, triangle, and other drums

55

Loving Spirit

Shirley Murray, New Zealand

I-to Loh, Taiwan

Lo - ving Spi - rit, lo - ving Spi - rit,
you have cho - sen me to be;___ you have drawn me
to___ your won - der,___ you have set your sign on me.___

Geist der Lie - be, Geist___ der Lie - be,
du hast mich ge - ru - fen: Sei!___ Du hast mich ans
Licht___ ge - zo - gen,___ hast dein Zei - chen ein - ge - setzt.___

Es - prit de Dieu ad - mi - ra - ble,
tu m'as choi - si(e), en - voie - moi.___ Tu m'at - ti - res,
tu___ me con - duis___ vers la beau - té___ de___ tes lois.___

DRUM

English

1 Loving Spirit, loving Spirit,
   you have chosen me to be;
   you have drawn me to your wonder,
   you have set your sign on me.

2 Like a mother, you enfold me,
   hold my life within your own,
   feed me with your very body,
   form me of your flesh and bone.

3 Like a father, you protect me,
   teach me the discerning eye,
   hoist me up upon your shoulder,
   let me see the world from high.

4 Friend and lover, in your closeness
   I am known and held and blessed;
   in your promise is my comfort,
   in your presence I may rest.

5 Loving Spirit, loving Spirit,
   you have chosen me to be;
   you have drawn me to your wonder,
   you have set your sign on me.

German

1 Geist der Liebe, Geist der Liebe,
   du hast mich gerufen: Sei!
   Du hast mich ans Licht gezogen,
   hast dein Zeichen eingesetzt.

2 Mütterlich umarmst du mich,
   hältst mich an dir, Tag und Nacht,
   sei du selbst mir Kraft und Speise;
   ich bin ja dir gleich gemacht.

3 Wie ein Vater schützt du mich,
   gibst mir Einsicht und Verstand,
   nimmst mich hoch auf deine Schultern,
   lässt von dort mich sehn die Welt.

4 Freundschaftlich und voller Liebe
   kennst du mich und bist mir nah;
   Trost und Segen find ich bei dir,
   wo du bist, ist Frieden da.

5 Geist der Liebe, Geist der Liebe,
   du hast mich gerufen: Sei!
   Du hast mich ans Licht gezogen,
   hast dein Zeichen eingesetzt.
   tr. Wolfgang Leyk
   and Andreas Wöhle

French

1 Esprit de Dieu admirable,
   tu m'as choisi(e), envoie-moi.
   Tu m'attires, tu me conduis
   vers la beauté de tes lois.

2 Comm'une mère tu m'entoures,
   tenant ma vie dans tes mains,
   tu m'as formé(e) comme ton corps,
   tu m'as nourri(e) de ton pain.

3 Comm'un père tu me gardes,
   enseigne-moi à aimer
   la justice venant de toi,
   en tout lieu la contempler.

4 Ami aimé, auprès de toi
   je suis chéri(e) et béni(e);
   mon réconfort, ma promesse,
   c'est en toi que je revis.

5 Esprit de Dieu admirable,
   tu m'as choisi(e), envoie-moi.
   Tu m'attires, tu me conduis
   vers la beauté de tes lois.
   tr. Joëlle Gouël

56 | May the love of the Lord

Maria Ling
based on Numbers 6: 24–6

SOON TI
Swee Hong Lim, Singapore

May the love
Wei_____ yuan
Un - ser Herr

of the Lord rest u-pon your soul.
Shen di ai fu - wei ni di___ ling.
sei bei dir, sei - ne Lie - be bei dir.

May his love dwell in you through - out ev - ery___
Mei shi - ke ta di ai zhu zai ni xin -
Un - ser Herr tra - ge dich durch den lan - gen___

day.
-li.
Tag.

May his coun - ten - ance shine u - pon you
Ta di rong - guang zhao - yao ni
Got - tes An - ge - sicht mö - ge leuch - ten

and be gra - cious to you.
ci - ai ban - sui ni.
ü - ber dir im-mer - dar.

May his Spir - it
Wu - lun he - chu
Sei - ne Hand be -

be u - pon you as you leave this place.
ta di ling dou yong - yuan ban - sui ni.
-glei - te dich, nun da du uns ver - lässt.

Mandarin tr. Dong Li; German tr. Angelika Joachim

57

May your breath of love

Maggie Hamilton, England

KUMBA YAH 88 86
Trad., African American/Caribbean

May your breath of love warm our hope, may your
Gott, dein Lie - bes-hauch wär - me uns, Gott, dein
Que ton a - mour don - ne l'e - spoir, que ton
Tu gra - tui - to a-mor ál - ze - nos, tu gra -

breath of love warm our hope, may your
Lie - bes - hauch wär - me uns, Gott, dein
a - mour don - ne l'e - spoir, que ton
-tui - to a - mor ál - ze - nos, tu gra -

breath of love warm our hope and heal our bro - ken world.
Lie - bes-hauch wär - me uns und hei - le uns - 're Welt.
a - mour don - ne l'e - spoir d'un mon - de qui gué - rit.
-tui - to a-mor ál - ze - nos dé al mun - do sa - na - ción.

English

1 May your breath of love warm our hope,
   may your breath of love warm our hope,
   may your breath of love warm our hope
   and heal our broken world.

2 May your kiss of love thrill our hearts, …
   and heal our broken world.

3 May your whispered love quell our fears, …
   and heal our broken world.

4 May your spark of love fire our dreams, …
   to heal our broken world.

5 May your raging love stir our wills, …
   to heal our broken world.

6 May your flagrant love fuel our power, …
   to heal our broken world.

German

1 Gott, dein Liebeshauch wärme uns,
   Gott, dein Liebeshauch wärme uns,
   Gott, dein Liebeshauch wärme uns
   und heile uns're Welt.

2 Gott, dein Liebeskuss wecke uns, …
   und heile uns're Welt.

3 Gott, dein Liebeswort tröste uns, …
   und heile uns're Welt.

4 Gott, dein Liebesglanz führe uns, …
   und heile uns're Welt.

5 Gott, dein Liebeslicht leite uns, …
   und heile uns're Welt.

6 Gott, dein Liebesbrand leuchte uns, …
   und heile uns're Welt.
                              tr. Angelika Joachim
                              and Päivi Jussila

French

1 Que ton amour donne l'espoir,
   que ton amour donne l'espoir,
   que ton amour donne l'espoir
   d'un monde qui guérit.

2 Que par ton amour dans nos cœurs, …
   le monde soit guéri.

3 Viens chasser nos peurs, par amour, …
   le monde va guérir.

4 Viens combler nos vœux, par amour, …
   le monde va guérir.

5 Ton amour nous pousse en avant, …
   le monde va guérir.

6 Ton amour va nous rendre forts, …
   le monde va guérir.
                              tr. Marc Chambron

Spanish

1 Tu gratuito amor álzenos,
   tu gratuito amor álzenos,
   tu gratuito amor álzenos
   dé al mundo sanación.

2 Tu tan tierno amor tóquenos, …
   dé al mundo sanación.

3 Tu sereno amor cálmenos, …
   dé al mundo sanación.

4 Tu radiante amor guíenos, …
   dé al mundo sanación.

5 Tu infinito amor cólmenos, …
   dé al mundo sanación.

6 Tu pujante amor muévanos, …
   dé al mundo sanación.
                              tr. Martin Junge
                              and Marietta Ruhland

58

Musande Mambo Mwari

Mr Zata, Zimbabwe

Mu - sa - nde
Ho - ly
Hei - lig

Mu - sa
Ho -
Hei -

Mu - sa - nde, m'sa - nde, m'sa - nde Ma - mbo Mwa - ri.
Mu - sa - nde, m'sa - nde, m'sa - nde wa - ma - si -
Ho - ly, ho - ly, ho - ly Lord God Sa - ba - oth.
Ho - ly, ho - ly, ho - ly God, Al - migh - ty
Hei - lig, hei - lig, hei - lig, du Herr Ze - ba - oth.
Hei - lig, hei - lig, hei - lig, du All - mäch - ti -

- nde 1. De - nga na - pa - si
- ly 1. All hea - ven and earth
- lig 1. Him - mel und Er - de

zvi - ze - re ne -
ma - ni - fest your
sind voll dei - ner

- mba.
One.
- ger.

Mwa - ri wa - ma - si - mba.
Lord God, Al - migh - ty One.
Gott, du All - mäch - ti - ger.

- mbi - ri ye - nyu.
glo - ry, O God.
Herr - lich - keit, Gott.

2. Ngaa - ru - mbi - dzwe.
2. Praise be to God.
2. Preis sei dir Gott.

Mu - sa - nde.
Ho - ly.
Hei - lig.

Mwa - ri wa - ma - sim - ba.
Lord God, Al - migh - ty One.
Gott, du All - mäch - ti - ger.

- ba.
One.
- ger.

From bar 6:

HOSHO (SHAKER)

DRUM

100

Shona

Leader Musande
All Musande, m'sande, m'sande
    Mambo Mwari.
Leader Musande
All Musande, m'sande, m'sande
    wamasimba.

1 **Leader** Denga napasi
  All *Mwari wamasimba.*
  Leader zvizere nembiri yenyu.
  All *Mwari wamasimba.*

2 **Leader** Ngaarumbidzwe
  All *Mwari wamasimba.*
  Leader ari kumusorosoro.
  All *Mwari wamasimba.*

3 **Leader** Ngaakudziwe
  All *Mwari wamasimba.*
  Leader samutumwa waMwari.
  All *Mwari wamasimba.*

4 **Leader** Ngaarumbidzwe
  All *Mwari wamasimba.*
  Leader ari kumusorosoro.
  All *Mwari wamasimba.*

Leader Musande
All Musande, m'sande, m'sande
    Mambo Mwari.
Leader Musande
All Musande, m'sande, m'sande
    wamasimba.

English

Leader Holy
All Holy, holy, holy
    Lord God Sabaoth.
Leader Holy
All Holy, holy, holy
    God, Almighty One.

1 **Leader** All heaven and earth
  All *Lord God, Almighty One.*
  Leader manifest your glory, O God.
  All *Lord God, Almighty One.*

2 **Leader** Praise be to God.
  All *Lord God, Almighty One.*
  Leader In the highest sing hosanna.
  All *Lord God, Almighty One.*

3 **Leader** Thanks be to God.
  All *Lord God, Almighty One.*
  Leader Blessed is the Saviour who comes,
  All *Lord God, Almighty One.*

4 **Leader** Blessed is He,
  All *Lord God, Almighty One.*
  Leader coming in the name of the Lord.
  All *Lord God, Almighty One.*

Leader Holy
All Holy, holy, holy
    Lord God Sabaoth.
Leader Holy
All Holy, holy, holy
    God, Almighty One.

tr. Maggie Hamilton

German

Vorsänger Heilig
Alle Heilig, heilig, heilig,
    du Herr Zebaoth.
Vorsänger Heilig
Alle Heilig, heilig, heilig,
    du Allmächtiger.

1 **Vorsänger** Himmel und Erde
  Alle *Gott, du Allmächtiger.*
  Vorsänger sind voll deiner
    Herrlichkeit, Gott.
  Alle *Gott, du Allmächtiger.*

2 **Vorsänger** Preis sei dir Gott.
  Alle *Gott, du Allmächtiger.*
  Vorsänger Hosianna in der Höhe.
  Alle *Gott, du Allmächtiger.*

3 **Vorsänger** Dank sei dir Gott.
  Alle *Gott, du Allmächtiger.*
  Vorsänger Sei gelobet, du, der da kommt,
  Alle *Gott, du Allmächtiger.*

4 **Vorsänger** Sei gelobet,
  Alle *Gott, du Allmächtiger.*
  Vorsänger der da kommt im Namen
    des Herrn.
  Alle *Gott, du Allmächtiger.*

Vorsänger Heilig
Alle Heilig, heilig, heilig,
    du Herr Zebaoth.
Vorsänger Heilig
Alle Heilig, heilig, heilig,
    du Allmächtiger.

tr. Päivi Jussila

59

Na nzela na lola

Mwenze Kabemba

Trad., Democratic Republic of Congo

Na nze-la na lo-la to-ko-ta-mbo-la ma-le-mbe, Ma-
We fol-low the Lord a-long the grad-ual road to hea-ven And
So-lan-ge wir ge-hen auf den We-gen uns'-res Got-tes, ist

-le-mbe to-ko-ta-mbo-la. Ma-le-mbe,_____ ma-
know God's king-dom it will come. We know this,_____ we
Hoff-nung für die gan-ze Welt. So lasst uns nun auch be-

Ma-le-mbe,__ ma-
We know this,__ we
So lasst uns__ be-

-le-mbe,__ ma-le-mbe to-ko-ta-mbo-la.
know this,__ we know God's king-dom it will come.
-harr-lich__ die We-ge uns'-res Got-tes gehn.

-le-mbe,__
know this,__
-harr-lich__

Lingala

1 **Leader**   Na nzela na lola tokotambola malembe,
  All   Malembe tokotambola.
  Leader   Na nzela na lola tokotambola malembe,
  All   Malembe tokotambola.
  All   *Malembe, malembe, malembe tokotambola.*
         Malembe, malembe, malembe tokotambola.

2 **Leader**   Na nzela na lola tokoyemba na esengo,
  All   Malembe tokotambola.

3 **Leader**   Na nzela na lola tokoteya na esengo,
  All   Malembe tokotambola.

4 **Leader**   Na nzela na lola tokobondela masiya,
  All   Malembe tokotambola.

English

1 **Leader**   We follow the Lord along the gradual road to heaven
  All   And know God's kingdom it will come.
  Leader   We follow the Lord along the gradual road to heaven
  All   And know God's kingdom it will come.
  All   *We know this, we know this, we know God's kingdom it will come.*
         We know this, we know this, we know God's kingdom it will come.

2 **Leader**   As long as we hope, there is a future for creation,
  All   A future for the universe.

3 **Leader**   As long as we pray (thank) (sing), there is a future for creation,
  All   A future for the universe.

4 **Leader**   As long as we act (believe), there is a future for creation,
  All   A future for the universe.
        tr. Carolyn Kappauf (altd.)

German

1 **Vorsänger**   Solange wir gehen auf den Wegen uns'res Gottes,
  Alle   ist Hoffnung für die ganze Welt.
  Vorsänger   Solange wir gehen auf den Wegen uns'res Gottes,
  Alle   ist Hoffnung für die ganze Welt.
  Alle   *So lasst uns nun auch beharrlich die Wege uns'res Gottes gehn.*
         So lasst uns nun auch beharrlich die Wege uns'res Gottes gehn.

2 **Vorsänger**   Solange wir hoffen, gibt es Zukunft für die Erde,
  Alle   ja Zukunft für die ganze Welt.

3 **Vorsänger**   Solange wir beten (danken) (singen), gibt es Zukunft für die Erde,
  Alle   ja Zukunft für die ganze Welt.

4 **Vorsänger**   Solange wir handeln (glauben), gibt es Zukunft für die Erde,
  Alle   ja Zukunft für die ganze Welt.
        tr. Werner Eichel and R. Höcker (altd.)

60

Nú hverfur sól í haf

Sigurbjörn Einarsson

Þorkell Sigurbjörnsson, Iceland

Nú hverf - ur sól__ í haf og húm - ið kem - ur
The sun sets in__ the sea, di - mi - nish - ing__ the
Die Son - ne sinkt ins Meer, rot ist der Dämm' - rung

skjótt. Ég lof - a góð - an Guð, sem gef - ur dag__ og
light. I thank you God of grace, who gives us day__ and
Licht. Mein Lob, Gott, zu__ dir klingt, für Tag und Nacht dir

nótt, minn vök - u - dag, minn draum og nótt.
night, my work - ing day,__ my dream, my night.
singt, für Schla - fen, Wa - chen Dank dir bringt.

Icelandic

1 Nú hverfur sól í haf
og húmið kemur skjótt.
Ég lofa góðan Guð,
sem gefur dag og nótt,
minn vökudag, minn draum og nótt.

2 Þú vakir, faðir vor,
ó, vernda börnin þín,
svo víð sem veröld er
og vonarstjarna skín,
ein stjarna hljóð á himni skín.

3 Lát daga nú í nótt
af nýrri von og trú
í myrkri hels og harms
og hvar sem gleymist þú
á jörð, sem átt og elskar þú.

4 Kom, nótt, með náð og frið,
kom nær, minn faðir hár,
og leggðu lyfstein þinn
við lífsins mein og sár,
allt mannsins böl, hvert brot og sár.

English

1 The sun sets in the sea,
diminishing the light.
I thank you God of grace,
who gives us day and night,
my working day, my dream, my night.

2 You are awake, O God,
protecting life that's weak
in all the whole wide world.
The star of hope we seek,
the star of hope of heav'n we seek.

3 As day leads into night
let hope and life break through
where hate and sorrow reign,
where we're forgetting you,
on earth where we're forgetting you.

4 Come night with grace and peace,
be near us, God of love,
come with your healing pow'r
to all the pain of life,
to all the human pain of life.

tr. Per Harling

German

1 Die Sonne sinkt ins Meer,
rot ist der Dämm'rung Licht.
Mein Lob, Gott, zu dir klingt,
für Tag und Nacht dir singt,
für Schlafen, Wachen Dank dir bringt.

2 Du schläfst und schlummerst nicht,
behütest Tag und Nacht,
was klein ist und was schwach.
Lass leuchten dein Angesicht,
lass leuchten uns dein Angesicht.

3 Zu Ende geht der Tag.
Lass Frieden in uns sein.
Wo Hass und Trauer sind,
lass neues Leben sein,
lass neues Leben für alle sein.

4 Bleib bei uns diese Nacht,
sei nah mit deiner Gnad.
Wo Schmerz und Trennung sind,
da lass jetzt Frieden sein;
lass uns, du Heiland, nicht allein.

tr. Dietrich Werner

61

Nu sjunker bullret

Lars Thunberg   T. I. Haapalainen, Finland

Nu sjun - ker bull - ret och stres - sen släp - per.
Nyt me - lu tyyn - tyy, työn pai - ne laan - tuu.
As eve - ning falls, Lord, we lay our bur - dens
Der Lärm ver - ebbt, und die Last wird leich - ter.

Din äng - la - vakt vå - ra mö - dor bär.
En - ke - li kuor - maam - me kos - ket - taa.
in - to your wel - com - ing, car - ing hands.
Es kom - men En - gel und tra - gen mit.

O Gud, väl - sig - na med nat - tens vi - la
Yön le - po siu - naa, oi Her - ra, meil - le.
Bless us with rest in the hours that fol - low,
Gott, seg - ne al - le, die dir ver - trau - en.

det folk vars me - ning du en - sam är!
Si - nul - ta kan - sa - si toi - von saa.
re - new - ing hope - ful - ness through all lands.
Gib Nacht und Ru - he, wo man heut litt.

Swedish

1 Nu sjunker bullret och stressen släpper.
 Din änglavakt våra mödor bär.
 O Gud, välsigna med nattens vila
 det folk vars mening du ensam är!

2 Låt rätten blomma där orätt råder!
 Gör fången fri och bryt våldet ned!
 När natten faller, låt kyrkan vaka
 och mänskan hålla med mänskan fred!

Finnish

1 Nyt melu tyyntyy, työn paine laantuu.
 Enkeli kuormaamme koskettaa.
 Yön lepo siunaa, oi Herra, meille.
 Sinulta kansasi toivon saa.

2 Siis murra kahleet ja väärä valta!
 Suo kukkaan puhjeta oikeuden!
 Suo, että kirkko myös yössä valvoo
 sovinnon liekkinä kaikkien.

tr. T.I. Haapalainen and
Anna-Maija Raittila

English

1 As evening falls, Lord, we lay our burdens
 into your welcoming, caring hands.
 Bless us with rest in the hours that follow,
 renewing hopefulness through all lands.

2 Where there is wrong let your justice flourish;
 banish all violence, set prisoners free!
 And, though we sleep, let our hearts be watchful,
 sharing your vision of unity.

tr. Maggie Hamilton

German

1 Der Lärm verebbt, und die Last wird leichter.
 Es kommen Engel und tragen mit.
 Gott, segne alle, die dir vertrauen.
 Gib Nacht und Ruhe, wo man heut litt.

2 Lass Recht aufblühen, wo Unrecht umgeht.
 Mach die Gefang'nen der Willkür frei.
 Lass deine Kirche mit Jesus wachen
 und Menschen wirken, dass Friede sei.

tr. Jürgen Henkys

62

Nun danket alle Gott

Martin Rinckart

NUN DANKET   67 67 66 66
Johann Crüger

Nun dan - ket al - le Gott mit Her - zen, Mund und Hän - den,
Now thank we all our God, with hearts and hands and voi - ces,
Lou - ons le Cré - a - teur, chan - tons à Dieu lou - an - ges!
De bo - ca y co - ra - zón lo - ad al Dios del cie - lo,

der gros - se Din - ge tut an uns und al - len En - den,
who wond-rous things has done, in whom his world re - joi - ces;
Et joi - gnons no - tre voix au con - cert des saints an - ges!
pues dió - nos ben - di - ción, sa - lud, paz y con - sue - lo.

der uns von Mut - ter - leib und Kin - des - bei - nen an
who, from our moth - er's arms has blessed us on our way
Dès les bras ma - ter - nels il___ nous a pro - té - gés,
Tan só - lo a su bon - dad de - be - mos nues - tro ser;

un - zäh - lig viel zu gut bis hier - her hat ge - tan.
with count - less gifts of love, and still is ours to - day.
et jus - qu'au der - nier jour, il est no - tre ber - ger.
su san - ta vo - lun - tad nos guí - a por do - quier.

German

1 Nun danket alle Gott
  mit Herzen, Mund und Händen,
  der grosse Dinge tut
  an uns und allen Enden,
  der uns von Mutterleib
  und Kindesbeinen an
  unzählig viel zu gut
  bis hierher hat getan.

2 Der ewigreiche Gott
  woll uns bei unserm Leben
  ein immer fröhlich Herz
  und edlen Frieden geben
  und uns in seiner Gnad
  erhalten fort und fort
  und uns aus aller Not
  erlösen hier und dort.

3 Lob, Ehr und Preis sei Gott
  dem Vater und dem Sohne
  und Gott dem Heil'gen Geist
  im höchsten Himmelsthrone,
  ihm, dem dreiein'gen Gott,
  wie es im Anfang war
  und ist und bleiben wird
  so jetzt und immerdar.

English

1 Now thank we all our God,
  with hearts and hands and voices,
  who wondrous things has done,
  in whom his world rejoices;
  who, from our mother's arms
  has blessed us on our way
  with countless gifts of love,
  and still is ours today.

2 O may this bounteous God
  through all our life be near us,
  with ever joyful hearts
  and blessèd peace to cheer us;
  and keep us in his grace,
  and guide us when perplexed,
  and free us from all ills
  in this world and the next.

3 All praise and thanks to God
  the Father now be given,
  the Son, and him who reigns
  with them in highest heaven;
  the one eternal God,
  whom earth and heaven adore;
  for thus it was, is now,
  and shall be evermore.

tr. Catherine Winkworth

Original version of melody

(French and Spanish verses overleaf)

French

1 Louons le Créateur,
  chantons à Dieu louanges!
  Et joignons notre voix
  au concert des saints anges!
  Dès les bras maternels
  il nous a protégés,
  et jusqu'au dernier jour,
  il est notre berger.

2 Loué soit notre Dieu!
  Que notre vie entière
  tous nous vivions joyeux
  sous le regard du Père,
  qu'il nous tienne en sa grâce
  et nous guide toujours,
  nous garde du malheur
  par son unique amour.

3 De ce Dieu trois fois saint
  qui règne dans la gloire,
  chrétiens empressons-nous
  de chanter la victoire;
  son Royaume est aux cieux
  où, plein de majesté,
  il règne, seul vrai Dieu,
  de toute éternité.

tr. du Pasquier

Spanish

1 De boca y corazón
  load al Dios del cielo,
  pues diónos bendición,
  salud, paz y consuelo.
  Tan sólo a su bondad
  debemos nuestro ser;
  su santa voluntad
  nos guía por doquier.

2 Oh Padre celestial,
  danos en este día
  un corazón filial
  y lleno de alegría.
  Consérvanos la paz;
  tu brazo protector
  nos lleve a ver su faz
  en tu ciudad, Señor.

3 Dios Padre, Creador,
  con gozo te adoramos.
  Dios Hijo, Redentor,
  tu salvación cantamos.
  Dios Santificador,
  te honramos en verdad.
  Te ensalza nuestra voz,
  bendita Trinidad.

tr. Federico Fliedner

63 Nyame ne Sunsum, sian brao!

Caroline Rockson, Ghana

Nya - me ne Sun - sum, sian brao!
O Ho - ly Spi - rit, come down,
Komm, Got - tes Geist, komm her - ab!
Es - prit de Dieu,— des - cends
Es - pí - ri - tu de Dios, ven,

Be - ye w'an - wa - wa 'dwu - ma.
work in us all your won - ders.
Zeig dei - ne Wun - der - ta - ten!
ac - com - plir tes mer - veil - les.
y re - nue - va tu o - bra.

Nya - me ne Sun - sum, sian bra - o!
O Ho - ly Spi - rit, come down to
Komm, Got - tes Geist, komm her - nie - der!
Es - prit de Dieu,— des - cends pour
Es - pí - ri - tu de Dios, ven,—

Be - ye w'an - wa - wa 'dwu - ma.
work in us all your won - ders.
Zeig dei - ne Wun - der - ta - ten!
ac - com - plir tes mer - veil - les.
y rea - li - za tu o - bra.

English tr. Maggie Hamilton; German tr. Dieter Trautwein; French tr. Joëlle Gouël; Spanish tr. Federico Pagura

111

64

O healing river

Trad., African American

O heal - ing riv - er,_____ send down your
O Fluss des Le - bens,_____ bring dei - ne
Sour - ce qui gué - rit,_____ fais cou - ler
Fuen - te de vi - da,_____ en - vía las

wa - ters,_____ send down your wa - ters_____ up - on this
Flu - ten,_____ lass Was - ser strö - men_____ in die - ses
tes flots,_____ fais cou - ler tes flots_____ sur cet - te
a - guas,_____ en - vía las a - guas_____ so - bre la

land._____ O heal - ing riv - er,_____ send down your
Land._____ O Fluss des Le - bens,_____ dein Was - ser
ter - re._____ Sour - ce qui gué - rit,_____ fais cou - ler
tier - ra._____ Fuen - te de vi - da,_____ en - vía las

wa-ters / and wash the blood_____ from off__ the sand._____
hei - le / und schwemm die Trä-nen_____ vom See - len - grund._____
tes flots, / et net - toie le sang_____ de tou-tes nos guerres._____
a - guas, / la - va la san-gre_____ de la a - re - na._____

English

1 O healing river, send down your waters,
   send down your waters upon this land.
   O healing river, send down your waters
   and wash the blood from off the sand.

2 This land is parching, this land is burning,
   no seed is growing in the barren ground.
   O healing river, send down your waters.
   O healing river, send your waters down.

3 Let the seed of freedom awake and flourish.
   Let the deep roots nourish, let the tall stalks rise.
   O healing river, send down your waters;
   O healing river from out of the skies.

German

1 O Fluss des Lebens, bring deine Fluten,
   lass Wasser strömen in dieses Land.
   O Fluss des Lebens, dein Wasser heile
   und schwemm die Tränen vom Seelengrund.

2 Das Land vertrocknet, versengt, verdurstet,
   kein grüner Grashalm auf dürrem Grund.
   O Fluss des Lebens, bring deine Fluten,
   dein Wasser fliesse, o Lebensstrom.

3 Die Saat der Freiheit lass keimen, wachsen,
   und tief verwurzelt lass sie erblühn.
   O Fluss des Lebens, mach neu die Erde,
   dein Wasser ströme aus Himmelshöh'n.
   tr. Horst Bracks

French

1 Source qui guérit, fais couler tes flots,
   fais couler tes flots sur cette terre.
   Source qui guérit, fais couler tes flots,
   et nettoie le sang de toutes nos guerres.

2 Dure est notre terre où tout est brûlé,
   pas un grain ne pousse sur son sol durci.
   Source qui guérit, fais couler tes flots,
   fais couler tes flots, source qui guérit.

3 Que la liberté puisse enfin fleurir
   pour que ses racines soient plus profondes.
   Source qui guérit, fais couler tes flots,
   que tombe la pluie du ciel sur le monde.
   tr. Marc Chambron

Spanish

1 Fuente de vida, envía las aguas,
   envía las aguas sobre la tierra.
   Fuente de vida, envía las aguas
   lava la sangre de la arena.

2 La tierra gime, la tierra arde,
   nada florece en tal hoguera.
   Fuente de vida, envía las aguas
   fuente eterna, danos la vida.

3 La libertad, oh, haz germinar,
   profundas raíces, produzcan flores.
   Fuente de vida, envía las aguas
   fuente eterna, abre los cielos.
   tr. Martin Junge

65

O God, we call

O GOD WE CALL 86 88
Words and music by
Linnea Good, Canada

French tr. Marc Chambron; German tr. Dietrich Werner

66

O let us spread the pollen of peace (The pollen of peace)

Words and music by
Roger Courtney, Northern Ireland

♩ = 120

INSTRUMENT (ad lib.),
second time only

A7   D   Em   A7   D   G

O let us spread the pol-len of peace through-out our land;_____
O komm und trag den Sa-men des Frie - dens in die Welt._____
Al-lons se - mer les grai-nes de paix_ sur no - tre terre._____

D   A7   D   G   Asus   A7

__ let us spread the pol-len of peace through-out our land;_____ let us
__ Mit uns trag den Sa-men des Frie - dens in die Welt._____ Mit uns
__ Ré-pan-dons les grai-nes de paix_ sur no-tre terre._____ Ré-pan-

spread the pol-len of peace_ and make all con-flicts cease, let us
trag den Sa-men des Frie - - dens wo Un-frie-de herrscht. Mit uns
- dons les grai-nes de paix,_ et ar-rê-tons les guerres. Ré- pan-

spread the pol-len of peace_ through-out our land._____
trag den Sa-men des Frie - dens in die Welt._____
- dons les grai-nes de paix__ sur no-tre terre._____

Fine

O Christ has sown the seeds of love;_____ O
O Herr, du schenkst Ver-söh-nung uns._____ Du
Christ a se-mé par-tout l'a- mour._____ Sa

116

German tr. Angelika Joachim and Päivi Jussila; French tr. Marc Chambron

67 | O living water, refresh my soul

Words and music by
Rosalie Vissing, USA

118

Spi - rit of God.   Spi - rit of God.
Du Heil - 'ger Geist.   Du Heil - 'ger Geist.
Es - prit de Dieu.   Es - prit de Dieu.

English

O living water, refresh my soul.
O living water, refresh my soul.
Spirit of joy, Lord of creation,
Spirit of hope, Spirit of peace.

1 Spirit of God. Spirit of God.

2 O set us free. O set us free.

3 Come, pray in us. Come, pray in us.

German

Wasser des Lebens, erquicke mich.
Wasser des Lebens, erquicke mich.
Du Geist der Kraft, du Gott der Schöpfung.
Du Geist der Zeit, du Geist der Ruh.

1 Du Heil'ger Geist. Du Heil'ger Geist.

2 Befreie uns. Befreie uns.

3 Bete in uns. Bete in uns.
tr. Angelika Joachim
and Päivi Jussila

French

Toi, l'eau vivante, baigne mon âme.
Toi, l'eau vivante, rafraîchis-moi.
Esprit de joie, ô Dieu créateur,
Esprit d'espoir, Esprit de paix.

1 Esprit de Dieu. Esprit de Dieu.

2 Délivre-nous. Délivre-nous.

3 Tu pries en nous. Tu pries en nous.
tr. Marc Chambron

68
O Saint Esprit, viens sur nous

Bayiga Bayiga, Cameroon

O Saint Es - prit, viens___ sur nous,
Spi - rit of God, vi - sit us.
Komm, Heil' - ger Geist, komm___ zu uns.
Es - pí - ri - tu ven___ a nos.

♩ = 150

O Saint Es - prit, viens sur nous.
Spi - rit of God, vi - sit us.
Komm, Heil' - ger Geist, komm zu uns.
Es - pí - ri - tu ven a nos.

Com - ble - nous de tes___ fa - veurs.
With your bless - ings fill___ our lives.
Und dein Se - gen fül - le uns.
Llé - na - nos de tu___ gra - cia.

English tr. Maggie Hamilton; German tr. Dietrich Werner; Spanish tr. Dorli Schwab

69

Oré poriajú verekó

Trad. Guarani, Paraguay

1. O - ré po - ria - jú ve - re - kó, Ñan - de -
2. O - ré po - ria - jú ve - re - kó, Je - su -

-ya - ra. O - ré po - ria - jú ve - re - kó, Ñan-de - ya - ra.
-cris - to. O - ré po - ria - jú ve - re - kó, Je - su - cris - to.

(Lord, have mercy. Christ, have mercy.)

(Herr, erbarme dich. Jesus Christus, erbarme dich.)

(Seigneur, aie pitié de nous. Jésus-Christ, aie pitié.)

(Señor, ten piedad. Jesucristo, ten piedad.)

Guarania

121

70 | Ososŏ

based on 2 Corinthians 5: 17–20

Words and music by
Geonyong Lee, Korea

O - so - sŏ___ o - so - sŏ, pyŏng-hwa - ŭi___ im - gŭm
Come, now, O___ Prince of peace, make us one___ bo - dy.
Komm nun, Fürst des Frie - dens, ein uns zu dei-nem Lei - be,
Viens, viens, ô___ roi de paix et ras - sem - ble - nous,
Ven, Dios, Prín - ci - pe de paz, haz - nos un___ cuer - po;

u - ri - ga___ han - mom i - ru - ge ha - so - sŏ.
Come, O Lord___ Je - sus, re - con-cile your___ peo - ple.
komm, Herr Je - sus, komm, ver - söh - ne dir all___ dein Volk.
viens, viens, ô___ maî - tre, ré - con - ci - lie ton peu - ple.
ven, Se - ñor,___ Je - sús, y re-con - ci - lia a tu pue - blo.

Korean

1 Ososŏ ososŏ,
   pyŏnghwaŭi imgŭm
   uriga hanmom
   iruge hasosŏ.

2 Ososŏ ososŏ,
   sarangŭi imgŭm,
   uriga hanmom
   iruge hasosŏ.

3 Ososŏ ososŏ,
   chayuŭi imgŭm,
   uriga hanmom
   iruge hasosŏ.

4 Ososŏ ososŏ,
   tongilŭi imgŭm,
   uriga hanmom
   iruge hasosŏ.

English

1 Come, now, O Prince of peace,
  make us one body.
  Come, O Lord Jesus,
  reconcile your people.

2 Come, now, O God of love,
  make us one body.
  Come, O Lord Jesus,
  reconcile your people.

3 Come now and set us free,
  O God, our Saviour.
  Come, O Lord Jesus,
  reconcile all nations.

4 Come, Hope of unity,
  make us one body.
  Come, O Lord Jesus,
  reconcile all nations.

tr. Marion Pope

German

1 Komm nun, Fürst des Friedens,
  ein uns zu deinem Leibe,
  komm, Herr Jesus, komm,
  versöhne dir all dein Volk.

2 Komm, nun, Gott der Liebe,
  ein uns zu deinem Leibe,
  komm, Herr Jesus, komm,
  versöhne dir all dein Volk.

3 Komm, nun und befrei uns,
  denn du bist unser Retter,
  komm, Herr Jesus, komm,
  versöhne dir alle Völker.

4 Komm, erhoffte Einheit,
  ein uns zu einem Leibe,
  komm, Herr Jesus, komm,
  versöhne dir alle Völker.

tr. Dieter Trautwein
and Dietrich Werner

French

1 Viens, viens, ô roi de paix
  et rassemble-nous,
  viens, viens, ô maître,
  réconcilie ton peuple.

2 Viens, viens, ô roi d'amour
  et rassemble-nous,
  viens, viens, ô maître,
  réconcilie ton peuple.

3 Viens, viens, libérateur
  et libère-nous,
  viens, viens, ô maître,
  réconcilie ton peuple.

4 Viens, viens, source d'espoir
  fais de nous ton corps,
  viens, viens, ô maître,
  réconcilie les peuples.

tr. Robert Faerber

Spanish

1 Ven, Dios, Príncipe de paz,
  haznos un cuerpo;
  ven, Señor, Jesús,
  y reconcilia a tu pueblo.

2 Ven, Dios, Príncipe de Amor,
  haznos sólo un cuerpo;
  ven, Señor Jesús,
  y reconcilia a tu pueblo.

3 Ven, Señor, liberanos
  Oh, Dios, Salvador;
  ven, Señor Jesús,
  y reconcilia a tu pueblo.

4 Fuente de esperanza, Dios,
  haznos sólo un cuerpo;
  ven, Señor Jesús,
  y reconcilia a tu pueblo.

tr. Martin Junge

71

Ouve, Senhor, eu estou clamando (Tem piedade)

based on Psalm 102: 1–2

Unknown, Brazil

Ou - ve, Se - nhor,_____ eu es - tou cla - man - do,_____
Hear me, O Lord,_____ O_ hear my cry - ing;_____
Hö - re mich, Herr,_____ wenn ich zu dir ru - fe._____
Pi - tié, Sei - gneur,_____ c'est vers toi que je crie,_____

— tem pie - da - de de mim e me res - pon - de.
in your mer - cy give ear to me and an - swer.
Hö - re mich, sei mir gnä - dig in Be - dräng - nis.
En - tends ma voix, ré - ponds à ma pri - è - re.

English tr. Alan Luff; German tr. Päivi Jussila

72

Porque él entró (Tenemos esperanza)

Federico J. Pagura, Argentina

Homero Perera, Uruguay

Spanish

1 Porque él entró en el mundo y en la historia;
porque él quebró el silencio y la agonía;
porque llenó la tierra de su gloria;
porque fue luz en nuestra noche fría;
porque él nació en un pesebre oscuro;
porque él vivió sembrando amor y vida;
porque partió los corazones duros
y levantó las almas abatidas.
Por eso es que hoy tenemos esperanza;
por eso es que hoy luchamos con porfía;
por eso es que hoy miramos con confianza
el porvenir en esta tierra mía.
Por eso es que hoy tenemos esperanza;
por eso es que hoy luchamos con porfía;
por eso es que hoy miramos con confianza
el porvenir.

2 Porque atacó a ambiciosos mercaderes
y denunció maldad e hipocresía;
porque exaltó a los niños, las mujeres,
y rechazó a los que de orgullo ardían.
Porque él cargó la cruz de nuestras penas
y saboreó la hiel de nuestros males;
porque aceptó sufrir nuestra condena
y así morir por todos los mortales.

3 Porque una aurora vió su gran victoria
sobre la muerte, el miedo, las mentiras;
ya nada puede detener su historia,
ni de su Reino eterno la venida.

Tango ensemble: piano, bandonéon (accordion), guitars

English

1 Because he came into our world and story,
   because he heard our silence and our sorrow;
   because he filled the whole world
        with his glory,
   and came to light the darkness
        of our morrow;
   because his birth was in a darkened corner,
   because he lived proclaiming life and love;
   because he quickened hearts that
        had been dormant,
   and lifted those whose lives had
        been down-trodden:
   so we today have hope and expectation,
   so we today can struggle with conviction,
   so we today can trust we have a future,
   so we have hope in this our world of tears.
   So we today have hope and expectation,
   so we today can struggle with conviction,
   so we today can trust we have a future,
   so we have hope.

2 Because he drove the merchants
        from the temple,
   denouncing evil and hypocrisy;
   because he raised up little ones and women,
   and put down all the mighty from their seats;
   because he bore the cross for our wrongdoings,
   and understood our failings and our weakness;
   because he suffered from our condemnation
   and then he died for every mortal creature:

3 Because of victory one morning early,
   when he defeated death and fear and sorrow,
   so nothing can hold back his mighty story
   nor his eternal kingdom tomorrow:
        tr. Len Lythgoe

German

1 In unser Leben, in uns're Geschichte
   ist er gekommen, sie mit uns zu teilen,
   und hat das Schweigen,
        hat die Angst zerbrochen
   und uns're Dunkelheit
        in Licht verwandelt.
   In einem unbekannten Stall geboren,
   um Liebe auszusäen und neues Leben,
   erstarrte Herzen endlich zu erweichen
   und die zu stützen, die am Boden liegen.
   Und darum sind wir heute voller Hoffnung,
   und darum kämpfen wir heut' ohne Zittern,
   und darum blicken wir heut' voll Vertrauen,
   in eine neue Zukunft für uns alle.
   Und darum sind wir heute voller Hoffnung,
   und darum kämpfen wir heut' ohne Zittern,
   und darum blicken wir heut' voll Vertrauen
   auf das, was kommt.

2 Gegen den Ehrgeiz der Geschäftemacher
   hat er gekämpft, und gegen jede Lüge,
   den Frauen, Kindern eig'nen Wert gegeben,
   aber die stolz und hart sind abgewiesen.
   Er trug mit uns das Kreuz all uns'rer Schmerzen
   und litt wie wir die Qual all uns'rer Übel,
   war selbst bereit, der Menschen Schuld zu teilen,
   um so den Tod für immer zu besiegen.

3 Weil uns're Welt dies Zeichen seiner Macht sah
   über den Tod, die Angst und alle Lügen,
   ist heute schon sein Wirken unaufhaltsam
   und wird auf Dauer niemals unterliegen.
        tr. Claudia Lohff Blatezky

73

Praise the God of all creation

Words and music by
Marty Haugen, USA

Praise the God of all cre - a - tion, God of mer-cy and com - pas - sion:
Lasst uns lo - ben un-sern Schöp-fer, Gott so gü - tig und barm - her - zig:
Sois bé - ni, ô Dieu du mon-de, toi, dont la grâ-ce est fé - con - de:

Al - le - lu - ia! Al - le - lu - ia! Praise the Word of truth and life! life!
Hal-le - lu - ja! Hal-le - lu - ja! Got - tes Wort schenkt Le - bens - kraft. - kraft.
Al - lé - lu - ia! Al - lé - lu - ia! Ta Pa - ro - le est no - tre joie. joie.

English

1   **Leader**   Praise the God of all creation, God of mercy and compassion:
     All   *Alleluia! Alleluia! Praise the Word of truth and life!*

2   Tree of life and endless wisdom, be our root, our growth and glory:

3   Living water, we are thirsting for the life that you have promised:

4   Come, O Spirit, kindle fire in the hearts of all your people:

5   Praise the God of all creation, God of mercy and compassion:

German

1   **Vorsänger**   Lasst uns loben unsern Schöpfer, Gott so gütig und barmherzig:
     Alle   *Halleluja! Halleluja! Gottes Wort schenkt Lebenskraft.*

2   Lebensbaum, wir wollen wachsen, in Gott wurzeln und vertrauen:

3   Gott, wir dürsten nach dem Wasser, das uns Leben neu verheisst:

4   Komm, erfüll uns, Geist des Lebens, mit dem Feuer deiner Vollmacht:

5   Lasst uns loben unsern Schöpfer, Gott so gütig und barmherzig:
         tr. Dorothea Wulfhorst

French

1   **Solo**   Sois béni, ô Dieu du monde, toi, dont la grâce est féconde:
     Tous   *Alléluia! Alléluia! Ta Parole est notre joie.*

2   Tu donnes vie et sagesse, sois notre force sans cesse:

3   Eau vivante, jaillissante, en nous source bienfaissante:

4   Viens habiter, par l'Esprit Saint, dans le cœur de tous les humains:

5   Sois béni, ô Dieu du monde, toi, dont la grâce est féconde:
         tr. Marc Chambron

74

Praise the One who breaks the darkness

Rusty Edwards

NETTLETON 87 87D
Unknown, USA

Praise the One who breaks the dark-ness with a li-ber-a-ting light;
Lob sei dir: All un-ser Dun-kel machst du hell mit dei-nem Licht.

praise the One who frees the pris-'ners, turn-ing blind-ness in-to sight.
Lob sei dir: Wer tief ge-fang-en, wer blind, er-lan-get ne-ue Sicht.

Praise the One who preached the gos-pel, heal-ing ev-'ry dread dis-ease,
Lob sei dir: die fro-he Bot-schaft, tie-fe Hei-lung du uns bracht,

calm-ing storms and feed-ing thou-sands with the ve-ry bread of peace.
gros-se Stür-me und den Hun-ger viel-er hast du still ge-macht.

English

1 Praise the One who breaks the darkness with a liberating light;
   praise the One who frees the pris'ners, turning blindness into sight.
   Praise the One who preached the gospel, healing ev'ry dread disease,
   calming storms and feeding thousands with the very bread of peace.

2 Praise the One who blessed the children with a strong yet gentle word;
   praise the One who drove out demons with a piercing, two-edged sword.
   Praise the One who brings cool water to the desert's burning sand;
   from this well comes living water quenching thirst in ev'ry land.

3 Praise the one true love incarnate: Christ, who suffered in our place.
   Jesus died and rose for many that we may know God by grace.
   Let us sing for joy and gladness, seeing what our God has done.
   Praise the one redeeming glory; praise the One who makes us one.

German

1 Lob sei dir: All unser Dunkel machst du hell mit deinem Licht.
   Lob sei dir: Wer tief gefangen, wer blind, erlanget neue Sicht.
   Lob sei dir: Die frohe Botschaft, tiefe Heilung du uns bracht,
   grosse Stürme und den Hunger vieler hast du still gemacht.

2 Lob sei dir: Den kleinen Kindern galt dein zartes Segenswort.
   Lob sei dir: Die dunklen Mächte durch dein Machtwort ziehen fort.
   Lob sei dir: Die trocknen Wüsten lässt du ergrünen zu voller Pracht.
   Durst nach Leben findet Antwort in dem Leben, das du schenkst.

3 Lob sei dir, du wahre Liebe: Christus, der für uns gelitten.
   Jesus starb und ist erstanden, dass wir neu erkennen Gott.
   Lasst uns jubeln, lasst uns singen, spüren, was Gott in uns tut.
   Lob sei dir: du schenkst uns Freiheit. Lob sei dir, du machst uns eins.
                    tr. Dietrich Werner

75 | Put peace into each other's hands

Fred Kaan, Netherlands/England

Ron Klusmeier, Canada

Put peace____ in - to____ each oth - er's hands__ and like____ a trea - sure hold it, pro - tect it like____ a can - dle flame, with ten - der - ness en - fold it.____

Legt Frie - den ein - an - der in__ die Hand,__ und wie____ ein Schatz__ be - schützt ihn, be - wahrt ihn wie____ ein Ker - zen - licht, mit Zärt - lich - keit ihn ent - fal - tet.____

English

1 Put peace into each other's hands
and like a treasure hold it,
protect it like a candleflame,
with tenderness enfold it.

2 Put peace into each other's hands
with loving expectation;
be gentle in your words and ways,
in touch with God's creation.

3 Put peace into each other's hands
like bread we break for sharing;
look people warmly in the eye:
our life is meant for caring.

Alternative (original) verses 4 and 5

4 Give thanks for strong—yet tender—hands,
held out in trust and blessing.
Where words fall short, let hands speak out,
the heights of love expressing.

4 As at communion, shape your hands
into a waiting cradle;
the gift of Christ receive, revere,
united round the table.

5 Reach out in friendship, stay with faith
in touch with those around you.
Put peace into each other's hands:
the Peace that sought and found you.

5 Put Christ into each other's hands,
he is love's deepest measure;
in love make peace, give peace a chance,
and share it like a treasure.

German

1 Legt Frieden einander in die Hand,
und wie ein Schatz beschützt ihn,
bewahrt ihn wie ein Kerzenlicht,
mit Zärtlichkeit ihn entfaltet.

3 Legt Frieden einander in die Hand,
wie Brot, das einander wir teilen.
Seht Menschen freundlich ins Angesicht,
begegnet einander in Liebe.

2 Legt Frieden einander in die Hand,
voll Hoffnung und Erwartung,
gewaltfrei sei euer Wort und Werk,
es achte Gottes Schöpfung.

4 Dank sei für jede off'ne Hand
entgegengestreckt dem Fremden.
Wo Worte fehlen, lasst Hände sprechen,
ein Zeichen setzen für Frieden.

5 In Freundschaft bleibt euch zugewandt,
im Glauben fest verbunden.
Legt Frieden einander in die Hand,
den Frieden, den Gott lässt wachsen.

tr. Dietrich Werner

76

Rakanaka Vhangeri

Trad. Shona, Zimbabwe

Shona

1 Rakanaka Vhangeri, rakanaka.
Rakanaka Vhangeri, rakanaka.
Rakanaka Vhangeri, rakanaka.
Rakanaka Vhangeri, rakanaka.
Nda nguri ndakuudza kuti rakanaka.
Nda nguri ndakuudza kuti rakanaka.
Nda nguri ndakuudza kuti rakanaka.
Nda nguri ndakuudza kuti rakanaka.

2 Rinesimba Vhangeri, rinesimba.
Rinesimba Vhangeri, rinesimba.
Nda nguri ndakuudza kuti rinesimba. ...

3 Ngariende Vhangeri, ngariende.
Ngariende Vhangeri, ngariende.
Nda nguri ndakuudza kuti ngariende. ...

English

1 Come and hear now the gospel, hear the good news.
Come and hear now the gospel, hear the good news.
Come and hear now the gospel, hear the good news.
Come and hear now the gospel, hear the good news.
We sing it many times again, the gospel's good news.
We sing it many times again, the gospel's good news.
We sing it many times again, the gospel's good news.
We sing it many times again, the gospel's good news.

2 Powerful is the gospel, very powerful.
Powerful is the gospel, very powerful.
We sing it many times again, the gospel's powerful. ...

3 Let us live out the gospel, live the good news.
Let us live out the gospel, live the good news.
We sing it many times again, go, live the good news. ...

tr. Francis Brienan and Maggie Hamilton

German

1 Gottes Wort tut uns gut! Ja, es tut gut!
Gottes Wort tut uns allen gut! Ja, es tut gut!
Gottes Wort tut uns gut! Ja, es tut gut!
Gottes Wort tut uns allen gut! Ja, es tut gut!
Ich habe dir schon immerzu erzählt: Es tut gut!
Ich habe dir schon immerzu erzählt: Es tut gut!
Ich habe dir schon immerzu erzählt: Es tut gut!
Ich habe dir schon immerzu erzählt: Es tut gut!

2 Gottes Wort gibt uns Kraft! Ja, es gibt Kraft!
Gottes Wort gibt uns allen Kraft! Ja, es gibt Kraft!
Ich habe dir schon immerzu erzählt: Es gibt Kraft! ...

3 Gottes Wort ruft nach Boten! Ja, es ruft uns!
Gottes Wort ruft nach vielen Boten! Ja, es ruft uns!
Ich habe dir schon immerzu erzählt: Es ruft uns! ...

tr. Hendriks Mavunduse and Dieter Trautwein

137

77
Reamo leboga

Trad., Botswana

Re - a - mo le - - bo - ga, re - a - mo
We give our thanks_____ to God, we give our
Wir dan - ken un - - serm Gott, wir dan - ken
Mer - ci à toi,_____ Sei - gneur, mer - ci à

le - bo - ga, re - a - mo le - bo - ga mo - di - mo wa ro - na.
thanks to God, we give our thanks to God, we give thanks to our God.
un - serm Gott, wir dan - ken un - serm Gott, der Dank gilt un - serm Gott.
toi, Sei - gneur, mer - ci à toi, Sei - gneur, nous te ren - dons grâ - ce.

2. Ga a yo yo tshwa - nang le - we - na
3. Re - pho - lo si - tswe ke - we - na

siTswana

1 Reamo leboga,
  reamo leboga,
  reamo leboga
  modimo wa rona.

2 Ga a yo yo tshwanang lewena, …
  modimo wa rona.

3 Repholo sitswe kewena, …
  modimo wa rona.

English

1 We give our thanks to God,
  we give our thanks to God,
  we give our thanks to God,
  we give thanks to our God.

2 There is no-one like God, …
  there's no-one like our God.

3 We have been saved by God, …
  we've been saved by our God.

tr. I-to Loh

German

1 Wir danken unserm Gott,
  wir danken unserm Gott,
  wir danken unserm Gott,
  der Dank gilt unserm Gott.

2 Denn Gott ist niemand gleich, …
  niemand gleicht unserm Gott.

3 Wir sind durch Gott befreit, …
  befreit durch unsern Gott.

tr. Wolfgang Leyk

French

1 Merci à toi, Seigneur,
  merci à toi, Seigneur,
  merci à toi, Seigneur,
  nous te rendons grâce.

2 Aucun n'est comme toi, …
  comme toi, ô Seigneur.

3 C'est lui qui nous sauva. …
  C'est Dieu qui nous sauva.

tr. Joëlle Gouël

78

Sa harap ng pagkaing dulot mo

Rolando S. Tinio
based on Acts 14:17

LATOK
Francisco F. Feliciano, Philippines

Sa ha - rap ng pag - ka - ing du - lot mo___ sa___ a - min
With the grace of this day's food, that you lay___ be - fore us,
Das___ Mahl, uns be - rei - tet: ein___ Zei - chen dei - ner Gna - de,

wa - lang sa - wa ka - ming___ nag - pa - pa - sa - la - mat.
bless us still___ as we thank you with hearts___ o - ver - flow - ing.
un - sern Dank wir vor dich brin - gen, ein Se - gens - lied dir sin - gen,

Ang i - yong___ pat - nu - bay hi - ni - hi - ngi___ na - min,
And be - stow___ on___ us,___ Lord, the guid - ance that we yearn for,
führ und lei - te du uns Gott, dein Licht er - hel - le die - se Ta - ge,

hin-di man__ ka - mi__ ka - ra - - pat - da - pat.
and be made__ more worth - y, Lord,_____ our__ giv - er.
lass uns schme-cken dein Gü - te, lass Neu - es uns noch wa - gen.

Tagalog

1 Sa harap ng pagkaing dulot mo sa amin
   walang sawa kaming nagpapasalamat.
   Ang iyong patnubay hinihingi namin,
   hindi man kami karapatdapat.

2 Walang sawa sa amin, turo mong pag-asa
   kaya't sana'y diggin ang aming dalangin.
   Ang pagkaing dulot balutin ng grasya,
   nang ang buhay ko'y 'yong marapatin.

English

1 With the grace of this day's food, that you lay before us,
   bless us still as we thank you with hearts overflowing.
   And bestow on us, Lord, the guidance that we yearn for,
   and be made more worthy, Lord, our giver.

2 You have never abandoned those who seek your counsel;
   so we pray that this meal be a meal for the spirit.
   May we grow in wisdom with ev'ry day that passes,
   and be made deserving of your bounty.
                    tr. Rolando S. Tinio (altd.)

German

1 Das Mahl, uns bereitet: ein Zeichen deiner Gnade,
   unsern Dank wir vor dich bringen, ein Segenslied dir singen,
   führ und leite du uns Gott, dein Licht erhelle diese Tage,
   lass uns schmecken dein Güte, lass Neues uns noch wagen.

2 Das Mahl, uns bereitet: ein Zeichen deiner Treue,
   wer sich zu dir völlig wendet, im Hunger niemals endet,
   führ und leite du uns Gott, dein Güte weite uns're Herzen,
   lass uns teilen die Gaben, mit and'ren uns laben.
                    tr. Dietrich Werner

79 | Salwalqulubi

from El Kasilik, Lebanon

English tr. John Campbell; German tr. Päivi Jussila; French tr. Marc Chambron; Spanish tr. Martin Junge

80

Santo es nuestro Dios

Words and music by
Guillermo Cuéllar, El Salvador

San - to, san - to, san - to, san - to, san - to, san - to es nues - tro Dios,
Ho - ly, ho - ly, ho - ly, ho - ly, ho - ly, ho - ly is our God,
Hei - lig, hei - lig, hei - lig, hei - lig, hei - lig, hei - lig un - ser Gott!
Trois fois saint est no - tre Pè - re, trois fois saint est no - tre Dieu.

Se - ñor de to - da la tie - rra, san - to, san - to es nues - tro Dios.
God of all the earth and hea - ven, ho - ly, ho - ly is our God.
Herr des Him - mels und der Er - de. Hei - lig, hei - lig un - ser Gott!
Sei - gneur de tou - te la ter - re; trois fois saint est no - tre Dieu.

144

English tr. Linda McCrae; German tr. Dieter Trautwein; French tr. Marc Chambron

Instruments: guitars, percussion

81 | Santo, santo, santo

Unknown, Argentina

Canción ♩ = 64

San - to,	san - to,	san - to.	!Mi	co - ra - zón	te a - do - ra!	Mi
Ho - ly,	ho - ly,	ho - ly.	With	joy my heart	a - dores you!	My
Hei - lig,	hei - lig,	hei - lig.	An -	be - tend stehn	wir vor dir.	Aus
Dieu saint,	Dieu saint,	Dieu saint!	Mon	cœur, mon cœur	t'a - do - re.	Mon

co - ra - zón	te	sa -	be de-cir:	!San - to e-rès	Se - ñor!
heart	cries out	to wor -	ship you:	Ho - ly are	you Lord!
vol - lem Her -	zen	ru -	fen_ wir:	Hei - lig bist	du, Gott!
cœur	le sait,	mon cœur	te le dit:	Sa - cré est	ton nom!

English tr. Maggie Hamilton; German tr. Dietrich Werner; French tr. Joëlle Gouël

82 Siyabonga

Trad., Southern/East Africa

English	**French**
Thank you, Jesus, amen.	Merci, Jésus, amen.
Thank you, Jesus, amen.	Merci, Jésus, amen.
Thank you, Jesus, amen.	Merci, Jésus, amen.
Alleluia, amen.	Alléluia, amen.
German	**Spanish**
Dank' sei dir, o Jesus.	Gracias, Jesús, amén.
Dank' sei dir, o Jesus.	Gracias, Jesús, amén.
Dank' sei dir, o Jesus.	Gracias, Jesús, amén.
Halleluja. Amen.	Aleluya, amén.

Seigneur, rassemble-nous

Words and melody by
Dominique Ombrie, France

Sei - gneur, ras-sem-ble - nous dans la paix de ton a - mour.
U - nite us, God, in peace and up - hold us with your love.
Im Frie - den mach uns eins, schenk uns dei - ne Lie - be, Herr!

Nos fau - tes nous sé - pa - rent, ta grâ - ce nous u -
Our faults di - vide and hin - der; your grace can make us
Es trennt uns uns' - re Sün - de, doch dei - ne Gna - de

- nit; la joie de ta vic - toi - re é - clai - re no - tre nuit.
one; we won-der at your ri - sing, your light is like the sun.
eint. Dein Sieg ist uns' - re Freu - de, er - leuch-tet uns' - re Nacht.

French

Seigneur, rassemble-nous
dans la paix de ton amour.

1 Nos fautes nous séparent,
ta grâce nous unit;
la joie de ta victoire
éclaire notre nuit.

2 Tu es notre espérance
parmi nos divisions;
plus haut que nos offenses
s'élève ton pardon.

3 Seigneur, vois la misère
des hommes affamés.
Partage à tous nos frères
le pain de l'unité.

4 Heureux le cœur des pauvres
qui cherchent l'unité!
Heureux dans ton royaume
les frères retrouvés.

5 Fais croître en notre attente
l'amour de ta maison;
l'Esprit dans le silence
fait notre communion.

6 Ta croix est la lumière
qui nous a rassemblés;
O joie de notre terre,
tu nous a rachetés.

7 La mort est engloutie,
nous sommes délivrés:
qu'éclate en nous ta vie,
Seigneur ressuscité!

English

Unite us, God, in peace
and uphold us with your love.

1 Our faults divide and hinder;
  your grace can make us one;
  we wonder at your rising,
  your light is like the sun.

2 You are our expectation
  in loneliness and pain;
  your healing and your pardon
  are greater than our sin.

3 Lord, look upon the starving
  and set the captive free.
  Share out among your children
  the bread of unity.

4 How happy are the people
  who strive to be at one,
  who learn to love each other,
  who lay their hatred down.

5 O God, whose silent spirit
  enlightens and endows,
  make us in faith receptive,
  and help us love your house.

6 Your cross will draw together
  the round of humankind;
  in you shall all the people
  their true communion find.

7 Death can no longer hurt us,
  triumphant is your word.
  Let life now grow and blossom,
  O Jesus, risen Lord!

tr. Fred Kaan

German

Im Frieden mach uns eins,
schenk uns deine Liebe, Herr!

1 Es trennt uns uns're Sünde,
  doch deine Gnade eint.
  Dein Sieg ist uns're Freude,
  erleuchtet unsre Nacht.

2 Du, Herr, bist uns're Hoffnung
  in der Zerrissenheit.
  Wir haben dich beleidigt,
  trotzdem verzeihst du uns.

3 Sieh, wie die Menschen leiden,
  am Hunger, der sie quält!
  Teil aus unter uns allen
  das Brot der Einigkeit!

4 Preist glücklich alle Armen,
  die auf der Suche sind!
  Preist glücklich alle Menschen,
  die zu dir heimgekehrt!

5 Lass in uns allen wachsen
  die Liebe für dein Reich!
  Dein Geist wirkt in der Stille
  Gemeinschaft unter uns.

6 Dein Kreuz wirft helle Strahlen,
  die haben uns vereint.
  O Glück, weil du die Erde
  uns wieder lieben lehrst!

7 Der Tod ist jetzt verschlungen,
  wir Menschen sind befreit!
  Durchdringe unser Leben,
  du auferstand'ner Herr!

tr. Marlies Flesch-Thebesius

84 | Señor, ten piedad de nosotros

Words and music by
Clara Ajo and Pedro Triana, Cuba

(Lord, have mercy. Christ, have mercy.)

(Herr, erbarme dich. Jesus Christus, erbarme dich.)

(Seigneur, aie pitié. Jésus-Christ, aie pitié.)

Percussion: sticks

qiu lian min— wo men.
Have— mer - cy on us.
er - bar - me dich.
ô prends pi - tié de nous.

Shang di de gao— yang,
O———— Lamb of God,
O———— Got - tes Lamm,
O toi, l'A-gneau de Dieu,

ni shi chu qu— shi ren zui nie de,
you take a - way— the sin of the world.
du nimmst hin - weg— die Sün-de der Welt;
toi qui en - lè - ves le pé-ché du monde,

qiu ci wo men ping an.
Grant— us— your peace.
gib uns Frie - den.
viens nous don-ner ta paix.

German tr. Päivi Jussila; French tr. Marc Chambron

153

86

Silence my soul

Rabindranath Tagore, India

Francisco F. Feliciano, Philippines

Ostinato (words repeated in free rhythm)

mf

GONG

Silence my soul
Schweig still, mein Herz

Very slow, meditative, in free rhythm

HIGH BELL

Si - lence my Soul these trees are prayers
Schweig still, mein Herz, die Bäu - me beten.

Si - lence my Soul these trees are prayers
Schweig still, mein Herz, die Bäu - me beten.

I asked the Tree
Ich sprach zum Baum.

I asked the Tree
Ich sprach zum Baum:

Tell me___ a-bout God
Er - zähl___ mir von Gott!

Tell me___ a-bout God
Er - zähl___ mir von Gott!

Then it blos - - somed
Und er blüh - - te.

GONG

154

Ostinato – sung to the words 'Silence my soul', with each singer in free rhythm. Middle C may be added to the ostinato. The ostinato continues throughout until the final gong.

Within the repeats there is freedom to improvise rhythmically, and the voices may enter at different times, overlapping.

The first repeat should be made at least three times. The last phrase may be reserved for the conclusion. The repeat of the final phrase is optional.

Additional verses by Seong-Won Park
Based on the Creation story in Genesis, using the Chinese symbol of days

1 Silence my soul
  the sun is prayer
  I asked the sun
  Tell me about God
  Then it shined

2 Silence my soul
  the moon is prayer
  I asked the moon
  Tell me about God
  Then it glowed

3 Silence my soul
  the fire is prayer
  I asked the fire
  Tell me about God
  Then it surged

4 Silence my soul
  the water is prayer
  I asked the water
  Tell me about God
  Then it rippled

5 Silence my soul
  the tree is prayer
  I asked the tree
  Tell me about God
  Then it blossomed

6 Silence my soul
  the tool is prayer
  I asked the tool
  Tell me about God
  Then it toiled

7 Silence my soul
  the earth is prayer
  I asked the earth
  Tell me about God
  Then it gave life

87

Strengthen for service, Lord

Syriac Liturgy of Malabar
tr. Charles Humphries and Percy Dearmer

JESU DULCIS MEMORIA
Plainchant

Streng - then for ser - vice, Lord, the hands that ho - ly things have
Stär - ke im Dienst, Gott, die Hän - de, die zum Zeug - nis be -
Nos mains, Sei - gneur, ont pris ton pain qu'elles servent aus - si no -
Da fuer - za a las ma - nos, Se - ñor, pues lo sa - gra - do han

ta - ken; let ears that now have heard thy songs_____
- ru - fen. Und lass die Oh - ren, die hö - ren dein Wort,
- tre pro - chain; Nos o - reil - les t'ont en - ten - du,_____
te - ni - do; a - bre los oí - dos a to - do cla - mor,

3.

to cla - mour ne - ver wa - ken. A - - men._____
nicht Lü - ge und Falsch - heit sich öffnen. A - - men._____
qu'el - les t'é - cou - tent tou - jours plus. A - - men._____
pues han oí - do tus can - tos. A - - mén._____

English

1 Strengthen for service, Lord, the hands
that holy things have taken;
let ears that now have heard thy songs
to clamour never waken.

2 Lord, may the tongues which 'Holy' sang
keep free from all deceiving;
the eyes which saw thy love be bright,
thy blessed hope perceiving.

3 The feet that tread thy holy courts
from light do thou not banish;
the bodies by thy Body fed
with thy new life replenish. Amen.

German

1 Stärke im Dienst, Gott, die Hände,
die zum Zeugnis berufen.
Und lass die Ohren, die hören dein Wort,
nicht Lüge und Falschheit sich öffnen.

2 Die Zungen, die singen dir Lob,
befreie von Täuschung und Trug.
Die Augen, die sehn deine Liebe,
erleuchte in ihrer Sicht.

3 Die Füsse, die nachfolgen dir,
mögen nicht gehn in die Irre,
sondern die Gläubigen hier leiten,
dass sie weiterziehen in Pracht. Amen.
tr. Dietrich Werner

French

1 Nos mains, Seigneur, ont pris ton pain
qu'elles servent aussi notre prochain;
Nos oreilles t'ont entendu,
qu'elles t'écoutent toujours plus.

2 Nos langues chantent ton saint nom
qu'elles disent aussi ce qui est bon;
Et nos yeux ont vu ton amour
qu'ils le contemplent pour toujours.

3 Et que nos pieds, qui t'ont suivi,
ne se perdent pas dans la nuit;
Qu'ils conduisent tous les croyants
sur ton chemin resplendissant. Amen.
tr. Marc Chambron

Spanish

1 Da fuerza a las manos, Señor,
pues lo sagrado han tenido;
abre los oídos a todo clamor,
pues han oído tus cantos.

2 Luego de cantarte, Santo,
frena las lenguas de engaño
ojos que han visto tu gloria brillar,
vean la esperanza bendita.

3 Los pies que nos llevan acá,
no tropiecen en la noche;
sigan tus sendas por nuestro mundo,
llévennos a seguirte a tí. Amén.
tr. Martin Junge

88

Slava voveki Tsaryu

Trad., Russian

Trad., Russian melody
arr. Ludmila Garbuzova, Russia

♩ = 68

Sla - va vo - ve - ki Tsa - ryu nye -
Glo - ry to the God of cre - a - tion.
Eh - re sei dir Schöp - fer al - len Le - bens.

- byess - no - mu! Sla - va, sla - - - va!
Glo - ri - a, glo - ria, glo - ri - a!
Eh - re sei Gott, dem e - - wi - gen Gott.

Russian

1 Slava voveki Tsaryu nyebyessnomu!
Slava, slava!

2 Slava Eesusu Christu I Spaseetyelyu!
Slava, slava!

3 Slava voveki Sviatomu Dukhu!
Slava, slava!

4 Slava voveki Triyedyinomu Bogu!
Slava, slava!

German

1 Ehre sei dir Schöpfer allen Lebens.
Ehre sei Gott, dem ewigen Gott.

2 Ehre sei dir Christus, Herr und Bruder,
Retter und Heiland für alle Welt.

English

1 Glory to the God of creation.
Gloria, gloria, gloria!

2 Glory to the Lord Jesus Christ
and Saviour for ever. Praise the Lord!

3 Glory to the Spirit, Holy Spirit,
now and for ever, for ever.

4 Glory to the Trinity, praise the Trinity,
praise the Triune God!
tr. Julia Garbuzova

3 Ehre sei dir, Gott, du Geist des Lebens,
Heiliger Geist, der Leben schafft.

4 Ehre dem dreieinigen, lebend'gen Gott.
Ehre sei Gott, dem ewigen Gott.
tr. Dietrich Werner

89

Te ofrecemos nuestros dones

Edwin Mora, Costa Rica
based on 1 Peter 4: 10,11

Walter Vivares, Argentina

Zamba ♩ = 146

E   B7

Te o - fre - ce - mos nues - tros do - nes al ser -
Te o - fer - ta - mos nos - sos dons ao ser -
Lord, ac - cept the gifts we bring you for the
Herr, wir brin - gen uns' - re Ga - ben, um dein

E   E7/G#

-vi - cio de tu rei - no. Te o - fre - ce - mos nues - tra
-vi - ço do teu Rei - no; te o - fer - ta - mos nos - sa
ser - vice of your king - dom; use our lives, our faith, our
Reich hier auf - zu - bau - en. Herr, wir brin - gen un - ser

A   B7   E

vi - da por tu cau - sa y por tu a - mor.
vi - da por tua cau - sa e teu a - mor.
ta - lents to make real your peace, your love.
Le - ben, weil du selbst die Lie - be bist.

Portuguese tr. Simei Monteiro; English tr. Fred Kaan; German tr. Dorothea Wulfhorst

LIGHT DRUM

GUITAR

90

Tembea na Yesu

Trad. Swahili, Kenya

(Walk with Jesus.)

(Geh mit Jesus!)

(Marchons avec Jésus!)

(Camina con Jesús.)

91 Thuma mina

Trad. Zulu, South Africa

(1. Send me, Lord. 2. I agree, Lord. 3. Thank you, Lord.)

(1. Sende mich, Herr. 2. Ich bin bereit, Herr. 3. Danke, Herr.)

(1. Prends-moi, Seigneur. 2. J'accepte, Seigneur. 3. Merci, Seigneur.)

(1. Envíame, Señor. 2. Estoy listo/a, Señor. 3. Gracias, Señor.)

92
The deer longs for pure flowing streams

George Mulrain, Trinidad
based on Psalm 42

Trad., Caribbean

The deer longs for pure flow-ing
Wie der Hirsch lechzt nach fri - schem

streams;   my thirst - y soul longs for the Lord: I have been weep-ing all day and all
Wasser   so schreit mei-ne See - le zu dir.   Mei - ne Trä-nen sind Spei-se für

night, for they say,   'Tell us, when will your God keep his word?'
mich Tag und Nacht, denn sie sa - gen: Wo ist nun dein Gott?

English

The deer longs for pure flowing streams;
my thirsty soul longs for the Lord:
I have been weeping all day and all night, for they say,
'Tell us, when will your God keep his word?'

So why are you downcast, my soul;
and why are you crying alone?
You must remember to put all your trust in your God,
and to praise him for what he has done.

By day the Lord shows me his love,
his blessings surround me at night:
so I will tell out his faithfulness, sing of his grace,
and, rejoicing, I'll walk in his light!

German

Wie der Hirsch lechzt nach frischem Wasser
so schreit meine Seele zu dir.
Meine Tränen sind Speise für mich Tag und Nacht,
denn sie sagen: Wo ist nun dein Gott?

Was zagest du so, meine Seele
und bist so unruhig in mir.
Harre auf Gott, denn du wirst ihm noch danken,
dass er Hilfe ist, Rat und mein Gott.

Am Tage zeigt Gott seine Güte,
des Nachts sing und bet ich zu ihm.
So will ich singen und danken dem lebend'gen Gott,
dass er Hilfe ist, Rat und mein Gott.
tr. Dietrich Werner

The Great Thanksgiving
Holy, holy, holy Lord

LAND OF REST
Trad., USA

Ho - ly, ho - ly, ho - ly Lord,___ God of pow-er and might;_____
Hei - lig, hei - lig, hei - lig, Herr,___ Gott, all-mächt-i - ger Herr._____

heaven and earth_ are full of your glo - ry. Ho - san - na in__ the high - est.
Al - le Land_ sind voll dei-ner Eh - re. Ho - sian - na in__ der Hö - he.

Bless - ed_ is he who comes in the name of the Lord.___ Ho -
Hochge - lobt_ sei, der da kommt im Na - men_ des Herrn.___ Ho -

-san - na in___ the high - est,___ ho - san - na in___ the high - est.
-sian - na,___ ho - sian - na,___ ho - sian - na in___ der Hö - he.

German tr. Päivi Jussila

(Saint, saint, saint est l'Éternel, Dieu de l'univers! Le ciel et la terre sont remplis de ta gloire. Hosanna au plus haut des cieux. Béni soit celui qui vient au nom du Seigneur. Hosanna au plus haut des cieux.)

(Santo, santo, santo es el Señor, Dios del universo. Llenos están el cielo y la tierra de tu gloria. Hosanna en el cielo. Bendito el que viene en el nombre del Señor. Hosanna en el cielo.)

93b
Christ has died

Christ has died.___ Christ is ris - en.___ Christ will come a - gain._____
Chris - tus starb,___ ist er - stan - den,_ kommt in Herr - lich - keit._____

Christ has died.___ Christ is ris - en.___ Christ will come a - gain.___
Chris - tus starb,___ ist er - stan - den,_ kommt in Herr - lich - keit.___

German tr. Angelika Joachim

(Christ est mort. Christ est ressuscité. Christ reviendra.)

(Cristo ha muerto. Cristo ha resucitado. Cristo vendrá otra vez.)

93c
Amen

A - men,___ a - men,_ a - - - men.___

94

Tú eres amor

Words and music by
Teresita Savall, Argentina

Canon

Tú e - res a - mor, tú e - res bon - dad, Se -
You, Source of all love, you, Giv - er of good, O
Die Lie - be ist dein, die Gü - te ist dein. Um
Toi, qui es l'a - mour, toi, qui es bon - té. Sei -

- ñor, da - nos la paz, que el mun - do no pue - de dar.
God, grant us your peace, the peace that the world can't give.
Frie - den bit - ten wir: Der Frie - den kommt stets von dir.
- gneur, don - ne la paix que seul tu peux nous don - ner.

English tr. Fred Kaan; German tr. Dorothea Wulfhorst; French tr. Marc Chambron

GUITAR

95

Those who wait upon the Lord

based on Isaiah 40: 31

Trad., North America

♩ = 66

INSTRUMENT (ad lib.)

D   F#m   Bm   A   A7   D

Those who wait u - pon the Lord shall re - new their strength,
Die auf ih - ren Herrn ver - traun, schöp-fen neu - e Kraft.

Em   A   A7   D   D7

they shall mount up on wings as ea - gles._____
Er ver - leiht Flü - gel wie den Ad - lern,_____

G   Em   F#m   Bm

They shall run and not be wea - ry, they shall walk and not faint.
dass sie lau - fen, nicht er - mü-den, dass sie gehn vol - ler Kraft.

Em   A7   D

Help us, Lord, help us, Lord, in your way._____
Hilf uns, Herr, hilf uns, Herr, auf dem Weg._____

English

1 Those who wait upon the Lord
   shall renew their strength,
   they shall mount up on wings as eagles.
   They shall run and not be weary,
   they shall walk and not faint.
   Help us, Lord, help us, Lord, in your way.

2 Those who serve a suff'ring world …

3 Those who sow the seeds of hope …

4 Those who work for peace on earth …

German

1 Die auf ihren Herrn vertraun
   schöpfen neue Kraft.
   Er verleiht Flügel wie den Adlern,
   dass sie laufen, nicht ermüden,
   dass sie gehn voller Kraft.
   Hilf uns, Herr, hilf uns, Herr, auf dem Weg.

2 Die bereit zum Dienen sind …

3 Die die Saat der Hoffnung sä'n …

4 Die die Saat des Friedens sä'n …
   tr. Angelika Joachim

(Ésaie 40: 31 Ceux qui espèrent dans le Seigneur retrempent leur énergie: ils prennent de l'envergure comme des aigles, ils s'élancent et ne se fatiguent pas, ils avancent et ne faiblissent pas!)

(Isaías 40: 31. Pero los que confían en el Señor tendrán siempre nuevas fuerzas y podrán volar como las águilas; podrán correr sin cansarse y caminar sin fatigarse.)

96

Truth is our call

Words and music by
Rima Nasir Tarazi, Palestine

Truth is our call and jus-tice our claim. The will of our God is our
Wahr-heit und Recht, da-zu du uns rufst. Des Le-bens__ Ziel nur dein

van-guard and aim; the God of us all, of mer-cy and love, of
Wil-le be-stimmt. Du Gott al-ler Menschen, voll Lie-be und Gnad, der

free-dom and peace for all of hu-man-kind.
Frei-heit und Frie-den will für je-des Kind.

We'll strive and we'll strive and we will not be still
Wir müh'n uns und kämp-fen und ge-ben nicht auf,

to lift all op-pres-sion with God's__ help and will.
bis Un-recht, Ge-walt, Un-ter-drü-ckung find ein End,

We'll raise high the ban - ner of right - eous-ness and truth,
dass al - les am En - de zum Gu - ten sich noch wend.

we'll strive and we'll strive and we will not be still.
Wir müh'n uns, zu än - dern was am Wel - ten Lauf.

English

1 Truth is our call and justice our claim.
  The will of our God is our vanguard and aim;
  the God of us all, of mercy and love,
  of freedom and peace for all of humankind.
  We'll strive and we'll strive and we will not be still
  to lift all oppression with God's help and will.
  We'll raise high the banner of righteousness and truth,
  we'll strive and we'll strive and we will not be still.

2 We shall not give in to fear or to hate;
  we will speak the truth and we'll strive to be just.
  With love we will stir the conscience of the world;
  with patience and faith we'll save our home and land.

German

1 Wahrheit und Recht, dazu du uns rufst.
  Des Lebens Ziel nur dein Wille bestimmt.
  Du Gott aller Menschen, voll Liebe und Gnad,
  der Freiheit und Frieden will für jedes Kind.
  Wir müh'n uns und kämpfen und geben nicht auf,
  bis Unrecht, Gewalt, Unterdrückung find ein End,
  dass alles am Ende zum Guten sich noch wend.
  Wir müh'n uns, zu ändern was am Welten Lauf.

2 Frei macht uns Gott von Angst oder Hass.
  Sein Recht, seine Wahrheit ist unser Mass.
  Mit Liebe verwandeln wir diese Welt.
  Geduld und Hoffnung unser Land erhält.
  tr. Dietrich Werner

97

Tua Palavra na vida

Words and music by
Simei Monteiro, Brazil

Tu - a   Pa - la - vra   na   vi - - - da
Es   tu   Pa - la - bra en   la   vi - - - da
Your   Word   in   our   lives,   e - ter - - - nal,
Dein   Wort   er - füllt   sich   im   Le - - - ben:

G9　　Abdim　　G7　　C6

é fon - te que ja - mais se - - - ca,
fuen - te que nun - ca se se - - - ca,
it is a clear foun - tain flow - - - ing;
Quel - le, die nie - mals ver - trock - - - net,

Dm　　F6　　Am7　　Am

á - gua que a - ni - ma e res - tau - - - ra
a - gua que a - ni - ma y res - tau - - - ra
wa - ter that gives strength and cou - - - rage
Was - ser, die Kräf - te zu we - - - cken

to intro.

Bbmaj7　　E7　　Am

to - dos que a quei - ram be - ber._____
a quie - nes quie - ran be - ber._____
to all who draw near and drink._____
je - dem, der nah - kommt und trinkt._____

(verses overleaf)

Portuguese

1 Tua Palavra na vida
é fonte que jamais seca,
água que anima e restaura
todos que a queiram beber.

2 Tua Palavra na vida
é qual semente que brota;
torna-se bom alimento,
pão que não há de faltar.

3 Tua Palavra na vida
é espelho que bem reflete,
onde nos vemos, sinceros,
como a imagem de Deus.

4 Tua Palavra na vida
é espada tão penetrante
que revelando as verdades
vai renovando o viver.

5 Tua Palavra na vida
é luz que os passos clareia,
para que ao fim no horizonte
se veja o Reino de Deus.

Spanish

1 Es tu Palabra en la vida
fuente que nunca se seca,
agua que anima y restaura
a quienes quieran beber.

2 Es tu Palabra en la vida
como semilla que brota;
llega a ser buen alimento,
pan que no nos faltará.

3 Es tu Palabra en la vida
espejo que bien refleja,
donde nos vemos, sinceros,
como la imagen de Dios.

4 Es tu Palabra en la vida
espada tan penetrante
que revelando verdades
va renovando el vivir.

5 Es tu Palabra en la vida
luz que los pasos aclara
y al fin, en el horizonte,
nos muestra el Reino de Dios.
tr. Jorge Rodríguez
and Pablo Sosa

English

1 Your Word in our lives, eternal,
it is a clear fountain flowing;
water that gives strength and courage
to all who draw near and drink.

2 Your word in our lives, eternal,
seed of the Kingdom that's growing;
it becomes bread for our tables,
food for the feast without end.

3 Your word in our lives, eternal,
becomes the mirror where we see
the true reflection of ourselves:
children and image of God.

4 Your word in our lives, eternal,
it is a sharp two-edged sword;
dividing our lies from your truth,
it's bringing new life to all.

5 Your word in our lives, eternal,
is light that shines on the long road
that leads us to the horizon
and the bright Kingdom of God.
tr. Sonya Ingwersen

German

1 Dein Wort erfüllt sich im Leben:
Quelle, die niemals vertrocknet,
Wasser, die Kräfte zu wecken
jedem, der nahkommt und trinkt.

2 Dein Wort erfüllt sich im Leben:
Samen, der keimt, sich entfaltet.
Nahrung, die froh wir empfangen,
Brot, das uns niemals mehr fehlt.

3 Dein Wort erfüllt sich im Leben:
Spiegel, darin uns zu schauen,
aufrichtig jetzt zu begreifen,
alle schuf Gott als sein Bild.

4 Dein Wort erfüllt sich im Leben:
Schwert, das tief eindringt und scharf ist,
Wahrheit, die weh tut, ans Licht bringt,
Leben erneuert und heilt.

5 Dein Wort erfüllt sich im Leben:
Licht, das die Schritte uns hell macht,
lässt uns, was kommt, klar erkennen,
ewig wird währen dein Reich.
tr. Dieter Trautwein

98

Utukufu

Trad. kiSwahili, Kenya

♩ = 112

LEADER ALL

Utu - ku - fu   Utu - ku - fu kwa mu - ngu   juu
Sing glo - ry!   Glo - ry be to God___ on   high.
Singt: Eh - re,   Eh - re sei dir in___ der   Höh.

LEADER ALL

A - ma - ni   A - ma - ni du___ ni - a - ni
Let peace reign!   Peace be to all___ cre - a - tion.
Singt: Frie - den,   Frie - den gibst du___ uns al - len.

LEADER ALL

K'we - nye ma - pe - nzi   K'we - nye ma - pe - nzi me - ma
Let love in - spire us!   Let love be gen - 'rous and full.
Du bist die Lie - be,   e - wi - ge Lie - be bist du.

LEADER ALL

K'we - nye ma - pe - nzi   K'we - nye ma - pe - nzi me - ma.
Let love in - spire us!   Let love be gen - 'rous and full.
Du bist die Lie - be,   e - wi - ge Lie - be bist du.

176

English tr. Fred Kaan; German tr. Angelika Joachim and Päivi Jussila

99

Våga vara den du i Kristus är

Anders Frostenson   Roland Forsberg, Sweden

Vå - ga va - ra den du i Kris - tus är,
Take the risk, be all that you are in Christ:
Wag's und sei doch, was du in Chri - stus bist,

den i hans tan - ke, den i hans kär - lek,
Christ in your think - ing, Christ in your lov - ing,
in sei - nem Ur - teil, in sei - ner Lie - be,

den i hans ö - gas e - vi - ga ljus du är.
let the tran - scen - dent light of your eyes be Christ's.
in sei - nes Au - ges e - wi - gem Licht schon bist!

Swedish

1 Våga vara den du i Kristus är,
  den i hans tanke,
  den i hans kärlek,
  den i hans ögas eviga ljus du är.

2 Intet äger du som ej han dig ger.
  Kravet och kraften,
  viljan och verket
  strömmar ur samma källa från
      bergen ner.

3 Skuld och rädsla trycker dig inte mer.
  Nu är du fri att
  älska och tjäna
  dem som du möter, Jesus som
      bor i dem.

4 Redan är du den du en gång skall bli:
  dömd och benådad,
  död och uppstånden,
  älskad och ett med honom som
      gjort dig fri.

English

1 Take the risk, be all that you are in Christ:
  Christ in your thinking,
  Christ in your loving,
  let the transcendent light of your eyes
      be Christ's.

2 Christ has given all that you have today:
  calling and courage,
  brave will and actions
  flow from the mountain-spring of the
      Christ always.

3 Shed the burden of all your guilt and fear;
  now you are free
  to love and to serve
  the stranger and neighbour: in them the
      Christ is here.

4 You are now all that you will one day be:
  judged and forgiven,
  dead and yet risen,
  cherished, and one with Christ who has
      set you free.
          tr. Maggie Hamilton

German

1 Wag's und sei doch, was du in Christus bist,
  in seinem Urteil,
  in seiner Liebe,
  in seines Auges ewigem Licht schon bist!

2 Gar nichts hast du, was er nicht selbst dir gab.
  Anspruch und Antwort,
  Wollen und Wirken
  strömen aus gleicher Quelle den Berg hinab.

3 Schuld und Ängste lasten nicht mehr auf dir.
  Nun bist du frei,
  zu dienen und lieben,
  wen du auch triffst und Jesus in ihm, in ihr.

4 Jetzt schon bist du, der einmal werden wird:
  schuldig und heilig,
  tot und erstanden,
  freigeliebt, eins mit Ihm, der dich heimgeführt.
          tr. Jürgen Henkys

100

Voice-over God, our Lover and Creator

Fred Kaan, Netherlands/England

Anfinn Øien, Norway

Voice - ov - er God, our Lov - er and Cre - a - tor,
Gott, der das Le - ben schuf, uns A - tem schenk - te,

whose Word trans - formed dis - or - der in - to peace,
der die - se Welt aus Chaos zum Frie - den rief.

who gave to all that is: a name, a call - ing,
Du kennst mit Na - men je - des Le - be - we - sen.

Words © 1985 Stainer & Bell Ltd

by whom all hu - man wis - dom was re - leased,
Voll dei - ner Weis - heit ist, was lebt und wirkt.

God! give us con - fi - dence in liv - ing, lov - ing,
Gott, gib uns Mut zu le - ben im Ver - trau - en,

the mind, the mood to make this life a feast.
das Le - ben sei ein Spie - gel dei - ner Gnad.

(*verses overleaf*)

English

1 Voice-over God, our Lover and Creator,
   whose Word transformed disorder into peace,
   who gave to all that is: a name, a calling,
   by whom all human wisdom was released,
   God! give us confidence in living, loving,
   the mind, the mood to make this life a feast.

2 Com-panion* Christ, in human terms among us,
   let your redeeming, freeing presence teach
   and help us not to measure those around us
   by culture, race, by gender, creed or speech,
   to look for that which is of God within them,
   reach out, give thanks, for what is good in each.

3 Ennobling Spirit, source of strength and passion,
   inspire our hearts to hear the voiceless cry,
   our will to break the shackles of injustice,
   take down all barriers that demean, divide;
   to give the hungry bread, the homeless shelter:
   life in all fullness, that will *never* die.

* Companion: from the Latin *cum* (together with) and *panis* (bread). A companion or a company is a person or persons with whom you share bread!

German

1 Gott, der das Leben schuf, uns Atem schenkte,
   der diese Welt aus Chaos zum Frieden rief.
   Du kennst mit Namen jedes Lebewesen.
   Voll deiner Weisheit ist, was lebt und wirkt.
   Gott, gib uns Mut zu leben im Vertrauen,
   das Leben sei ein Spiegel deiner Gnad.

2 Christ, unser Bruder, Mensch an uns'rer Seite,
   sei gegenwärtig mitten unter uns,
   dass weder Rasse, Religion noch Farbe
   verstell den Blick für Würde, Menschenrecht,
   dass wir dein Bild und deine Spur erkennen
   in jedem Menschen, den du liebst wie mich.

3 Geist, Gottes Kraft und Stärke auch im Leiden,
   mach unsere Herzen weit, wenn Stumme schrei'n,
   mach uns'ren Willen fest, ein Nein zu sagen,
   zu allem Unrecht, allem, was uns trennt,
   Brot sei dem Hungrigen und Schutz gegeben,
   so dass von Lebensfülle alle spür'n.
                 tr. Dietrich Werner

101
Vai com Deus!

Words and music by
Simei Monteiro, Brazil

Samba ♩ = 92

Vai com Deus!	Ain-da é ma - dru - ga - da_ nas ru - as da ci -	-da - de,_
Go with God!	It is al - most dawn in_ the still streets of the	ci - ty,_
Geh mit Gott!	Bei An - bruch des Mor - gens sind stil - le noch die	Stras - sen._
Ve con Dios!	Aún es ma - dru - ga - da!_ ni un al - ma por la	ca - lle,_

e com su - a bên - ção,_	va - mos com Deus!
as we feel your bless - ings,	we go in peace!
Gott ist mit uns heu - te,_	er bleibt bei uns.
si Dios nos ben - di - ce _	va - mos con Él.

Não se sa - be a - in - da_ se tu - do vai dar cer - to,_	
No - thing is for cer - tain,_ the day is still a mys - tery,_	
Nichts ist si - cher für uns,_ der Tag ist noch ver - bor - gen._	
Y aun - que no sa - be - mos_ có - mo an - da - rán las co - sas,_	

mas se Deus nos gui - a vai i - lu - mi - nar._____	
trust - ing in your grace, we know the light will come._____	
Wir ver - trau - en Gott, dem Herrn: Der Tag bricht an._____	
si el Se - ñor nos gui - a nos va i - lu - mi - nar!_____	

German tr. Päivi Jussila; Spanish tr. Pablo Sosa

Samba (in combination)

Instruments: guitars, percussion

102

Vos sos el destazado en la cruz

Words and music by
Carlos Mejia Godoy, Nicaragua

$\left.\right.$ = 78

Em · B · B7

Vos sos el des - ta - za-do en la cruz, que has ven - ci - do la
On the cross, when they put you to death, you de - feat-ed the
Al - le Schmer-zen trugst du selbst am Kreuz, das das Bö - se der

Em · B

mal-dad del mun - do,___ de - nun - cian-do al in - jus-to o-pres - sor,
for - ces of e - vil,___ you con - demned the op - pres-sors' in - justice,
Welt ü - ber - wun - den.___ Un - ter - drü-ckung hast du bloss-ge - stellt,

B7 · Em · Am

le - van - tan - do del pol-vo a los po - bres. Te pe - di - mos
raised the poor from the dust of de - press - ion. Hear our pro - test,
aus dem Staub auf - ge - rich-tet die Ar - men. Wir___ ru - fen,

Em · B7 · Em

que nos oi - gas,___ que es-cu - ches el cla - mor de tu pue - blo. Te pe -
heed our an - guish,___ and res - pond to the hopes of your peo - ple. Hear our
drän - gen, bit - ten,___ dass die Kla-gen du hörst dei - nes Vol - kes. Wir___

Am · Em · B7 · Em

- di - mos que nos oi - gas,___ que es-cu - ches el cla - mor de tu pue - blo.
pro - test, heed our an - guish,___ and res - pond to the hopes of your peo - ple.
ru - fen, drän - gen, bit - ten,___ dass die Kla-gen du hörst dei - nes Vol - kes.

Spanish

1 Vos sos el destazado en la cruz,
que has vencido la maldad del mundo,
denunciando al injusto opresor,
levantando del polvo a los pobres.
Te pedimos que nos oigas,
que escuches el clamor de tu pueblo.
Te pedimos que nos oigas,
que escuches el clamor de tu pueblo.

2 Vos sos el destazado en la cruz,
masacrado por los poderosos;
hoy derramas tu sangre también
en la sangre de nuestros caídos.
Te pedimos …

3 Vos sos el destazado en la cruz,
que construyes la paz con justicia.
Ayúdanos a no desmayar,
a luchar por que venga tu Reino.
Que tu paz llegue a nosotros
cuando hagamos brotar la justicia.
Que tu paz llegue a nosotros
cuando hagamos brotar la justicia.

English

1 On the cross, when they put you to death,
you defeated the forces of evil,
you condemned the oppressors' injustice,
raised the poor from the dust of depression.
Hear our protest, heed our anguish,
and respond to the hopes of your people.
Hear our protest, heed our anguish,
and respond to the hopes of your people.

2 On the cross, when they put you to death
(they—the merchants of ill and destruction),
you were one with all victims of torture,
loved ones, shedding their life-blood for others.
Hear our protest …

3 Yet the cross, where you died, is today
sign and symbol of life, peace and justice,
stands among us and calls us to service:
let your Kingdom of love rule creation!
Let your peace inspire, unite us
in pursuit of life's fullness and justice.
Let your peace inspire, unite us
in pursuit of life's fullness and justice.
                                   tr. Fred Kaan

German

1 Alle Schmerzen trugst du selbst am Kreuz,
das das Böse der Welt überwunden.
Unterdrückung hast du blossgestellt,
aus dem Staub aufgerichtet die Armen.
Wir rufen, drängen, bitten,
dass die Klagen du hörst deines Volkes.
Wir rufen, drängen, bitten,
dass die Klagen du hörst deines Volkes.

2 Alle Schmerzen trugst du selbst am Kreuz,
ein Opfer der Mächt'gen geworden.
Und das Blut, das gekostet dein Tod,
uns're Märtyrer heute verlieren.
Wir rufen …

3 Alle Schmerzen trugst du selbst am Kreuz,
durch das Frieden wächst in Recht und Freiheit.
Hilf, dass lähmend in uns nicht die Angst,
sondern stark unsere Hoffnung:
          dein Reich kommt!
Deinen Frieden gib uns heute,
dass wir bleiben die Zeugen des Rechtes.
Deinen Frieden gib uns heute,
dass wir bleiben die Zeugen des Rechtes.
                        tr. Dietrich Werner

103

Wa Emimimo

Deliberately ♩ = 80

ALL

The Church of the Lord (Aladura), Nigeria

Wa wa wa E - mi - mi - mo,
Come, O Ho - ly Spir - it, come,
Komm, o komm, Hei - li - ger Geist,
O viens, Es - prit,___ viens

LEADER

E - mi - o - lo - ye.
Ho - ly Spir - it, come.
Geist der Wahr - heit
Es - prit de sa - gesse

Wa wa wa A - lag - ba - ra,
Come, al - migh - ty Spir - it, come,
komm, o komm, du Geist voll Kraft,
O viens, puis - sant Es - prit, viens,

A - lag - ba - ra - me - ta.
al - might - y Spir - it, come.
du Geist der Ei - nig - keit,
Puis - san - te Tri - ni - té

Wa - o, wa - o, wa - o.___
Come,___ come,___ come.___
komm,___ komm,___ komm.___
viens,___ viens,___ viens.___

E - mi - mi - mo.
O Spir - it, come.
Hei - li - ger Geist.
O Es - prit, viens.

English tr. I-to Loh; German tr. Wolfgang Leyk; French tr. Joëlle Gouël

SHAKER

DRUM 1

DRUM 2
or GONG

104 | We believe, Maranatha

based on Revelation 22: 5,20

Francisco F. Feliciano, Philippines

German tr. Dieter Trautwein; French tr. Marc Chambron

105

We shall go out with hope of resurrection

June Boyce-Tillman, England

LONDONDERRY AIR
Trad., Northern Ireland

188

Words © 1993 Stainer & Bell Ltd

bold - ly,　　tales　of　a　love　　that will　not　let　us　go.＿＿＿＿　We'll sing our
Hoff-nung,　Bot-schaft der Liebe,　die nie-mand je-mals　aufgibt.＿＿＿＿　Wir sing'n das

songs　　　of　wrongs that　can　be　right　-　ed.　　We'll dream our
Lied,　　dass Un-recht wan-delt　sich ins Recht.　　Wir hal-ten

dreams of hurts that can be healed.___ We'll weave a cloth of all the world u-
fest den Traum, dass Wun-den heilen.___ Wir stri-cken wei - ter an dem Netz der

-ni - ted with-in the vi-sion of a Christ who sets us free.___
Hoff - nung, dass ei - ne Welt in Chris-tus wird, der macht uns frei.___

English

1 We shall go out with hope of resurrection;
  we shall go out, from strength to strength go on.
  We shall go out and tell our stories boldly,
  tales of a love that will not let us go.
  We'll sing our songs of wrongs that can be righted.
  We'll dream our dreams of hurts that can be healed.
  We'll weave a cloth of all the world united
  within the vision of a Christ who sets us free.

2 We'll give a voice to those who have not spoken.
  We'll find a word for those whose lips are sealed.
  We'll make the tunes for those who sing no longer,
  vibrating love alive in every heart.
  We'll share our joy with those who still are weeping,
  chant hymns of strength for hearts that break in grief.
  We'll leap and dance the resurrection story,
  including all within the circles of our love.

German

1 Wir stehen auf in der Kraft des Auferstand'nen,
  wir ziehen aus gestärkt durch seine Macht.
  Wir stehen auf mit Geschichten seiner Hoffnung,
  Botschaft der Liebe, die niemand jemals aufgibt.
  Wir sing'n das Lied, dass Unrecht wandelt sich ins Recht.
  Wir halten fest den Traum, dass Wunden heilen.
  Wir stricken weiter an dem Netz der Hoffnung,
  dass eine Welt in Christus wird, der macht uns frei.

2 Wir geben Stimme allen, denen das Wort verboten.
  Wir rufen laut für alle, die verstummt sind.
  Wir singen neu für alle, denen das Lied vergangen,
  dass Liebe wächst erneut in jedem Herz.
  Wir teilen Freude mit all denen, die noch weinen.
  Wir singen Lieder zu stärken, die voll Kummer.
  Wir tanzen, feiern das Fest des Auferstand'nen,
  weiten die Kreise unserer Liebe nach aussen hin.
        tr. Dietrich Werner

106
Wij geloven één voor één

Joke Ribbers   Bernard Smilde, Netherlands

Wij ge - lo - ven één voor één en ook sa - men:
We be - lieve, as one by one and to - ge - ther;
Lasst uns glau - ben ganz al - lein, und zu - sam - men,
C'est la foi de tout chré - tien, c'est la nô - tre:

de Heer is God en an - ders geen. A - men, a - men.
the Lord is God, there is none else, a - men, a - men.
dass Gott der Herr ist, nie - mand sonst. A - men. A - men.
Dieu tient le mon - de dans ses mains. A - men, a - men.

Dutch

1 Wij geloven één voor één
en ook samen:
de Heer is God en anders geen.
Amen, amen.

2 Wij geloven in de naam
Jezus Christus,
gestorven en weer opgestaan.
Halleluja!

3 Wij geloven dat de Geest
ook nog heden
de wereld en onszelf geneest.
Vrede, vrede.

English

1 We believe, as one by one
and together;
the Lord is God, there is none else,
amen, amen.

2 We believe in Jesus's name,
Christ among us,
condemned to death, but raised to life:
Alleluia!

3 We believe that even now
God the Spirit
will heal the world and heal us all:
Peace be with us!

tr. Fred Kaan

German

1 Lasst uns glauben ganz allein,
und zusammen,
dass Gott der Herr ist, niemand sonst.
Amen. Amen.

2 Lasst uns glauben Jesus Christ,
unser Heiland,
gestorben und erstanden ist.
Amen. Amen.

3 Lasst uns glauben, dass der Geist,
Geist des Lebens,
die Welt verwandelt und uns heilt.
Amen. Amen.

tr. Dietrich Werner

French

1 C'est la foi de tout chrétien,
c'est la nôtre:
Dieu tient le monde dans ses mains.
Amen, amen.

2 Nous croyons en Jésus-Christ,
mort sur la croix:
Pour toujours il a repris vie.
Alléluia!

3 Nous croyons en l'Esprit Saint,
qui, sans cesse,
vient pour guérir tous les humains,
et le monde.

tr. Marc Chambron

107

Word of justice (Litany of the Word)

Words and music by
Bernadette Farrell, England

English

1 Word of justice, *Alleluia,* come to dwell here. *Maranatha!*

2 Word of mercy, *Alleluia,* live among us. *Maranatha!*

3 Word of power, *Alleluia,* live within us. *Maranatha!*

4 Word of freedom, *Alleluia,* save your people. *Maranatha!*

5 Word of healing, *Alleluia,* heal our sorrow. *Maranatha!*

6 Word of comfort, *Alleluia,* bring us hope now. *Maranatha!*

7 Word of gladness, *Alleluia,* fill our hearts now. *Maranatha!*

8 Word of wisdom, *Alleluia,* come renew us. *Maranatha!*

German

1 Wort des Rechtes, *Halleluja,* nimm hier Wohnung. *Maranatha!*

2 Wort der Gnade, *Halleluja,* sei uns Leben. *Maranatha!*

3 Wort der Stärke, *Halleluja,* sei uns Beistand. *Maranatha!*

4 Wort der Freiheit, *Halleluja,* bring Erlösung. *Maranatha!*

5 Wort der Heilung, *Halleluja,* heile Wunden. *Maranatha!*

6 Wort des Trostes, *Halleluja,* stärke Hoffnung. *Maranatha!*

7 Wort der Freude, *Halleluja,* füll die Herzen. *Maranatha!*

8 Wort der Weisheit, *Halleluja,* komm, erneu're. *Maranatha!*

tr. Dorothea Wulfhorst

French

1 O Parole, *Alléluia,* viens parmi nous, *Maranatha!*

2 Tu pardonnes, *Alléluia,* tu te donnes, *Maranatha!*

3 Tu es force, *Alléluia,* et puissance, *Maranatha!*

4 Tu libères, *Alléluia,* tu nous sauves, *Maranatha!*

5 Ta guérison, *Alléluia,* nous l'attendons, *Maranatha!*

6 Tu consoles, *Alléluia,* nos tristesses, *Maranatha!*

7 Allégresses, *Alléluia,* et tendresse, *Maranatha!*

8 O sagesse, *Alléluia,* ô promesse, *Maranatha!*

tr. Marc Chambron

108

Xin Chua thuong xot chung con

Unknown, Vietnam

♩. = 48

LEADER
Xin Chu - a thuong xot___ chung con,
O Lord,___ your mer - cy show,___
Sei du___ uns gnä - dig, Herr.___

ALL
Xin Chu - a thuong xot___ chung con,
O Lord,___ your mer - cy show,___
Sei du___ uns gnä - dig, Herr.___

LEADER
Xin Chu - a Ki - to___ thuong xot___ chung con,
O Je - sus Christ,___ your mer - cy show,
Sei du___ uns gnä - dig, Je - su Christ.

ALL
Xin Chu - a Ki - to___ thuong xot___ chung con,
O Je - sus Christ,___ your mer - cy show,
Sei du___ uns gnä - dig, Je - su Christ.

LEADER
Xin Chu - a thuong xot___ chung con,___
O Lord,___ your mer - cy show,___
Sei du___ uns gnä - dig, Herr.___

ALL
Xin Chu - a thuong xot___ chung con.___
O Lord,___ your mer - cy show.___
Sei du___ uns gnä - dig, Herr.___

German tr. Inge Klaas

(Seigneur, aie pitié de nous. Jésus-Christ, aie pitié. Seigneur, aie pitié de nous.)

(Señor, ten piedad. Jesucristo, ten piedad. Señor, ten piedad.)

109 | Ya hamalaLah

Yusuf Khill, Palestine/Israel

♩ = 72

Ya_ ha-ma-la - Lah al-ha-mel kha-ta-yal - 'a_____ lam ir - ham____ na.
O_ Lamb of God, you take_ a - way the sins of the world, have mer-cy on us.
Du Got-tes-lamm nimmst hin-weg al - le Schuld auf Er - den, er - bar - me dich.

Ya_ ha-ma-la - Lah al - ha-mel kha-ta-yal - 'a_____ lam im -
O_ Lamb of God, you take _ a - way the sins_ of the world, grant
Du_ Got-tes-lamm nimmst hin - weg al - le Schuld aur Er - den, bring

-nah - na - sa-lam, im - nah - na - sa-lam, im - nah - na - sa - lam.
us your_ peace, grant us your_ peace, grant us_____ your peace.
Frie - den_ uns, bring Frie - den_ uns, bring Frie - den zu uns.

German tr. R. Renner and U. Schwendler

110

Yarabba ssalami

Unknown, Palestine

♩ = 78

Ya - ra - bba ssa - la - mi   am - ter a - lay - na ssa - lam,
God of peace, in your wis - dom   give us the will to seek peace;
Du Gott des Frie - dens,   giess dei - nen Frie - den auf uns,
Toi, Dieu de la paix   en - voie ta paix sur nous tous.
Tu, oh Dios, de la paz   da - nos a - mor por tu paz;

ya - ra - bba ssa - la - mi   im la' qu - lu - ba - na sa - lam.
God of peace and of heal - ing,   fill with your peace ev - ery heart!
du Gott des Frie - dens,   fül - le mit Frie-den un - ser Herz.
Toi, Dieu de la paix   com - ble nos cœurs de ta paix.
Tu, oh Dios, de la paz   en nues-tras vi - das siem-bra paz.

English tr. Fred Kaan; German tr. Renate Schiller; Spanish tr. Martin Junge

Sung unaccompanied, or with an oud or guitar playing the melody in repeated notes.

111

Zonse zimene n'za Chauta wathu

Trad. Chichewa, Malawi

(Everything belongs to our God. All power, everything good.)

(Alles gehört Gott. Alle Macht, alles Gute.)

(Tout appartient à notre Dieu. Toute puissance, toute bonté.)

(Todo pertenece a nuestro Dios. Todo poder, todo lo bueno.)

Chauta means 'owner of the rainbow'.
Chauta bedeutet 'dem der Regenbogen zu eigen ist'.
Chauta signifie 'propriétaire de l'arc en ciel'.
Chauta significa 'propietario del arco iris'.

Copyright Acknowledgements

The Publishers are grateful to those who have given permission for copyright material to be included. Every effort has been made to trace copyright owners, and apologies are extended to anyone whose rights have inadvertently not been acknowledged. Omissions or inaccuracies of copyright detail will be corrected if possible in subsequent printings.

Oxford University Press is a member of the Christian Copyright Licensing schemes; licence holders may reproduce copyrights controlled by OUP (and those of other copyright-owner members of CCL) under the terms of that scheme. Anyone outside the CCL scheme who wishes to reprint material administered by OUP should apply to the Copyright Administrator, Music Department, Oxford University Press, Great Clarendon Street, Oxford OX2 6DP.

An acknowledgement has been placed on the same page as a hymn where the copyright owner has requested this as a condition of granting permission. However, such on-page matter has been kept to a minimum, and users should refer to the complete list of copyright information which follows. A list of the main organizations which own copyrights reproduced in this book is given at the end of this list; for any information not included here, please write to Oxford University Press (as above), enclosing a reply-paid envelope.

1   Music transcription © Maggie Hamilton
2   Words © Ulises Torres, translations © (P) Jaci Maraschin, (E) Fred Kaan, (G) tvd-Verlag Düsseldorf, (Fr) Marc Chambron
3   Translations © (E) Fred Kaan, (G) Strube Verlag, (Fr) Lutheran World Federation
4   Music transcription © Alexander Lingas
5   Translations © (E) Emmanuel Badejo, (G) Horst Bracks
6a Translations © (Fr) Réveil Publications, (Sp) Frederico J. Pagura
6b German text © Edwin Nievergelt; translations © (Fr) Marc Chambron, (Sp) Simei Monteiro
8   Translations © (E) Fred Kaan, (G) Dietrich Werner, (Fr) Marc Chambron, (Sp) Lutheran World Federation
9   Translations © (E) Fred Kaan, (G) Strube Verlag, (Fr) Marc Chambron
10 Translations © (G) Dietrich Werner, (Fr) Marc Chambron
11 Music arrangement © Oxford University Press; words © D. Sealy, translations © (E) Oxford University Press, (G) Dietrich Werner
12 Music arrangement © Simei Monteiro & Oxford University Press; translations © (E) Gerhard Cartford, (G) Strube Verlag, (Fr) Marc Chambron
13 Music and words © Wild Goose Resource Group, translations © (G) Thomas Laubach, (Fr) Hans Schmocker
14 Music © William A. Cross; words © GIA Publications, translation © Dietrich Werner
15 Music transcription © Maggie Hamilton
16 Music and words © Per Harling; music arrangement © Terry MacArthur; translations © (E) Per Harling, (G,Sp) World Council of Churches, (Fr) Joëlle Gouël

17 Music and words © Merete Wendler; translations © (E) Fred Kaan, (G) Dietrich Werner
18 Music arrangement © Rimantas Sliuzinskas; translations © (E) Per Harling, (G) Dietrich Werner
19 Music and words © Sr. Adelheid Wenzelmann; translations © (E) Fred Kaan, (Fr) Marc Chambron, (G) Lutheran World Federation
20 Music and words © Ateliers et Presses de Taizé; translation © (Fr) Marc Chambron
21 Translations © (E) Fred Kaan, (G) Dietrich Werner
22 Music and words © Pablo Sosa; translations © (E) Pablo Sosa, (G) Strube Verlag
23 Music © Norsk Musikforlag
24 Music and words © Harold Flammer Music, a division of Shawnee Press, Inc.; translations © (G) Dorothea Wulfhorst, (Fr) Marc Chambron, (Sp) Lutheran World Federation
25 Words © 1968 Stainer & Bell; translations © (G) Strube Verlag, (Fr) Marc Chambron
26 Translations © (G) Strube Verlag, (Fr) World Council of Churches
27 Music © Ateliers et Presses de Taizé
29 Music © I-to Loh; words © Ruth Duck; translations © Lutheran World Federation
30 Music adaptation © Christian I. Tamaela
31 Music arrangement © Oxford University Press; words © Norman C. Habel; translations © (G) Dietrich Werner, (Fr) Marc Chambron
32 Music © Knut Nystedt; words © Sverre Therkelsen; translations © (E) Oxford University Press, (G) Sverre Therkelsen
33 Music and words © Olli Kortekangas; translations © (E) Oxford University Press, (G) Dietrich Werner, (Fr) Marc Chambron

Addresses of organisations owning copyrights reproduced in this book

Evangélikus Sajtoosztaly
c/o Evangelical Lutheran Church in Hungary
Szilagyi Erzsebet Fasor 24
1125 Budapest
Hungary

General Board of Global Ministries
GBGMusic
475 Riverside Drive
New York
NY 10115
USA

GIA Publications, Inc.
7404 South Mason Avenue
Chicago
IL 60638
USA

Kirkon Keskusrahasto
PO Box 185
FIN-00161 Helsinki
Finland

Lutheran World Federation
PO Box 2100
Route de Ferney 150
CH-1211 Geneva 2
Switzerland

Music Sales (Harold Flammer Inc.)
8–9 Frith Street
London
W1V 5TZ
United Kingdom

Norsk Musikforlag A/S
Postboks 1499 Vika
0116 Oslo
Norway

OCP Publications
5336 NE Hassalo
Portland
OR 97213
USA

Oxford University Press
Music Copyright Department
Great Clarendon Street
Oxford
OX2 6DP
United Kingdom

Réveil Publications
20 rue Calliet
BP 4464
F-69241 Lyon Cedex 04
France

Shalom Community Inc.
1504 Polk
Wichita Falls
Texas 76309
USA

Stainer & Bell Ltd
Victoria House
23 Gruneisen Road
London
N3 1DZ
United Kingdom

Strube Verlag
Pettenkoferstr. 24
D-80336 München
Germany

tvd-Verlag
Postfach 321111
D-40426 Düsseldorf
Germany

Universidad Biblico Latinoamericano
Calle 3
Avenidas 14 y 16 - Apdo. 901-1000
San José
Costa Rica

Vereinte Evangelische Mission
Rudolfstr. 137
D-42285 Wuppertal
Germany

Weltgebetstagskommittee, Stein
KlensVerlag GmbH
Postfach 320620
D-40421 Düsseldorf
Germany

Wild Goose Resource Group
Iona Community
Pearce Institute
840 Govan Road
Glasgow
G51 3UU
United Kingdom

Willow Connection Pty. Ltd
PO Box 341
Dee Why
NSW 2099
Australia

World Alliance of Reformed Churches
PO Box 2100
Route de Ferney 150
CH-1211 Geneva 2
Switzerland

World Council of Churches
PO Box 2100
Route de Ferney 150
CH-1211 Geneva 2
Switzerland

Zimbabwe Catholic Association of Sacred Music
PO Box CY 738
Causeway
Harare
Zimbabwe

Liturgical Index/Liturgischer Index/ Index liturgique/Índice litúrgico

This index contains suggestions of songs that might be used at particular points during the liturgy, reflecting a range of styles and traditions.

Dieser Index schlägt Lieder unterschiedlicher Stilrichtungen und Traditionen für verschiedene liturgische Zwecke vor.

Cet index suggère des cantiques, de styles et de traditions variés, qui peuvent être chantés aux différents moments de la liturgie.

Este índice contiene sugerencias de cantos de diversos estilos y tradiciones para ser usados en los diferentes momentos de la liturgia.

Acclamation/Akklamation/Acclamation/Aclamación

A ivangeli ya famba (1)	Mozambique
A Palavra do Senhor (3)	South America
E toru nga mea (21)	Aotearoa New Zealand
Praise the God of all creation (73)	USA
Rakanaka Vhangeri (76)	Zimbabwe
Siyabonga (82)	Southern/East Africa

Affirmation of faith/Glaubensbekenntnis/Affirmation de la foi/Afirmación de fe

Jikelele (40)	South Africa
Reamo leboga (77)	Botswana
We believe, Maranatha (104)	Philippines
Wij geloven één voor één (106)	Netherlands
Zonse zimene n'za Chauta wathu (111)	Malawi

Agnus Dei: Lamb of God/Lamm Gottes/Agneau de Dieu/Cordero de Dios

Jesus, Lamb of God (37)	USA
Lamb of God (47)	Canada
Shang di de gao yang (85)	China
Vos sos el destazado en la cruz (102)	Nicaragua
Ya hamalaLah (109)	Palestine/Israel

Alleluia/Halleluja/Alléluia/Aleluya

Aleluya Y'in Oluwa (5)	Nigeria
Alleluia (7)	Ukraine
Haleluya Puji Tuhan (30)	Indonesia
Iloitse, maa! (33)	Finland

Amen/Amen/Amen/Amén
The Great Thanksgiving (Amen) (93*c*)　　　　　　USA

Baptism/Taufe/Baptême/Bautismo
Crashing waters at creation (14)　　　　　　Canada
O healing river (64)　　　　　　African American
O living water, refresh my soul (67)　　　　　　USA

Blessing/Segen/Bénédiction/Bendición
Bwana awabariki (10)　　　　　　Tanzania
Komm, Herr, segne uns (45)　　　　　　Germany
May the love of the Lord (56)　　　　　　Singapore
Tú eres amor (94)　　　　　　Argentina
Yarabba ssalami (110)　　　　　　Palestine

Communion/Abendmahl/Communion/Comunión
Bendice, Señor, nuestro pan (9)　　　　　　Argentina
Du bist unser alles (19)　　　　　　Germany
Eat this bread (20)　　　　　　France
El cielo canta alegría (22)　　　　　　Argentina
Jesus, Lamb of God (37)　　　　　　USA
Jesus, Lamb of God, bearer of our sin (38)　　　　　　England
Let us break bread together (52)　　　　　　African American
Loving Spirit (55)　　　　　　Taiwan
Sa harap ng pagkaing dulot mo (78)　　　　　　Philippines

Confession of sins/Sündenbekenntnis/Confession du péché/Confesíon de pecados
A ti, Señor, te pedimos (2)　　　　　　Chile

Daily prayer/Stundengebet/Prière quotidienne/Oración diaria
asato maa sad gamaya (8)　　　　　　India
Kiedy ranne wstają zorze (44)　　　　　　Poland
La ténèbre (46)　　　　　　France
Le Seigneur fit pour moi des merveilles (49)　　　　　　France
Let my prayer rise before you (50)　　　　　　USA
Nú hverfur sól í haf (60)　　　　　　Iceland
Nu sjunker bullret (61)　　　　　　Finland
Vai com Deus! (101)　　　　　　Brazil
We believe, Maranatha (104)　　　　　　Philippines

Eucharistic prayer/Abendmahlsgebet/Prière eucharistique/Oración eucarística
The Great Thanksgiving (Christ has died) (93*b*)　　　　　　USA

Gathering/Eröffnung/Rassemblement/Al congregarse

All people that on earth do dwell (6*a*)
Come, Holy Spirit, descend on us (13)   Scotland

Gloria: **Glory to God/Ehre sei Gott/Gloire à Dieu/Gloria a Dios**

Gloria a Dios (26)   Peru
Gloria in excelsis Deo! (27)   France
Slava voveki Tsaryu (88)   Russia
Utukufu (98)   Kenya

Invocation/Anrufung/Invocation/Invocación

Come, Holy Spirit, descend on us (13)   Scotland
Dvasia Šventoji, ateiki (18)   Lithuania
Nyame ne Sunsum, sian brao! (63)   Ghana
O God, we call (65)   Canada
O Saint Esprit, viens sur nous (68)   Cameroon
Ososŏ (70)   Korea
Wa Emimimo (103)   Nigeria

Kyrie: **Lord, have mercy/Herr, erbarme dich/Seigneur, aie pitié/Señor, ten piedad**

Gospodi pomilui (28)   Ukraine
Khudaya, rahem kar (42)   Pakistan
Kyrie eleison (43)   Ghana
Oré poriajú verekó (69)   Paraguay
Señor, ten piedad de nosotros (84)   Cuba
Xin Chua thuong xot chung con (108)   Vietnam

Litany/Litanei/Litanie/Letanía

Word of justice (Litany of the Word) (107)   England

Offertory/Gabenbereitung/Offertoire/Ofertorio

Te ofrecemos nuestros dones (89)   Argentina

Our Father/Vaterunser/Notre Père/Padrenuestro

Fader vår (23)   Norway

Post-communion prayer/Dankgebet/Post-communion/Oración de Acción de Gracias

Strengthen for service, Lord (87)

Psalmody/Psalmodie/Psalmodie/Salmodia

All people that on earth do dwell (Psalm 100) (6*a*)
Cantai ao Senhor (Psalm 98) (12)   Brazil
Iloitse, maa! (Psalm 100) (33)   Finland

Laudate omnes gentes (Psalm 117) (48)   France
Let my prayer rise before you (50)   USA
The deer longs for pure flowing streams (Psalm 42) (92) Caribbean

Response/Antwortgesang/Réponse/Responsorio
For God alone (24)   Canada
I will live for you alone   (34)   Australia
Laudate omnes gentes (48)   France
Le Seigneur fit pour moi des merveilles (49)   France
Let my prayer rise before you (50)   USA
O God, we call (65)   Canada
Ouve, Senhor, eu estou clamando (71)   Brazil
Salwalqulubi (79)   Lebanon
We believe, Maranatha (104)   Philippines

Sanctus: Holy/Heilig/Saint/Santo
Du är helig (16)   Sweden
Musande Mambo Mwari (58)   Zimbabwe
Santo es nuestro Dios (80)   El Salvador
Santo, santo, santo (81)   Argentina
The Great Thanksgiving (Holy, holy, holy Lord) (93*a*)   USA

Sending/Sendung/Envoi/Envío
Tembea na Yesu (90)   Kenya
Those who wait upon the Lord (95)   North America
Thuma mina (91)   South Africa
Truth is our call (96)   Palestine
Vai com Deus! (101)   Brazil
We shall go out with hope of resurrection (105)   Northern Ireland

Table grace/Tischgebet/Prière pour le repas/Bendición de los alimentos
Be present at our table, Lord (Table graces) (6*b*)
Bendice, Señor, nuestro pan (9)   Argentina
Du bist unser alles (19)   Germany
Sa harap ng pagkaing dulot mo (78)   Philippines

The Peace/Friedensgruss/La paix/La paz
Put peace into each other's hands (75)   Canada

Trisagion: Holy God/Dreimalheilig (Heiliger Gott)/Dieu saint/Santo Dios
Agios o Theos (4)   Greece

Biblical References/Übersicht der Bibelstellen/ Références bibliques/Referencias bíblicas

First Lines and Titles/Liedanfänge und Titel/
Premières lignes et titres/Primeras líneas y títulos

Titles are shown in *italics*/Die Titel sind *kursiv* gedruckt/
Les titres apparaissent en *italiques*/Los títulos aparecen en *cursiva*